NOCITA CARTER

Personal Finance Tips For You

Tips You Can Use To Help You With Your Personal Finances

ISBN-13: 978-0-9823485-0-5
ISBN-10: 0-9823485-0-9

Library of Congress Control Number: 2009901321

Disclaimer

Published by WebLinks
P.O. Box 892125
Temecula, CA. 92589-2125

To order additional copies, please contact us.
BookSurge
www.booksurge.com
1-866-308-6235
orders@booksurge.com

TABLE OF CONTENTS

ACKNOWLEDGEMENTS

Personal Finance Tips For You is dedicated to anyone who believes that they are in need of tips and information to assist them with improving their personal finances.

Today we are living in difficult economic times. We are finding ourselves seeking as much information and assistance as we can to help us wither this financial storm. I want to thank all of you for giving me the opportunity and inspiration for creating this book for you.

INTRODUCTION

Your personal finances are very important to you especially in our current economic hard times. It seems as though we are continuing to hear daily about the huge number of people being layed off, companies that have become bankrupt, families loosing their homes to foreclosures, and now what we all have not wanted to be involved in and what we realistically know is we are in a recession. Some people also believe that we may be facing a depression. It's unclear what's ahead for us down the road so we must try to prepare ourselves the best way we can.

It is important to know as much as you can about managing your personal finances in these economic times. You want to be armed with as much information that can assist you in paving your way through our current economic storm. It will be difficult, but perseverance, determination, consistency and educating yourself more about your personal finances will be able to assist you in making it through.

Personal Finance Tips For You was created with you in mind. The tips in this book are provided to assist you with various personal finance topics that you may encounter. Tips on keeping you out of credit card traps, paying yourself first, protecting yourself against identity theft, staying on track to pay your bills on time, discussing finances before you get married and many more personal finance tips that may be able to help you.

So go ahead and get started with reading these tips that will hopefully assist you in becoming more knowledgeable about how to handle your own personal finances for today, tomorrow and for the future.

Chapter 1
Don't Get Caught Up In The Credit Card Trap, Stop Yourself Before That Happens!

That's right don't get caught up in the trap of never paying off your high interest credit cards! Or, for that matter all of your credit cards. It's so important to pay off your credit cards, especially the high interest rate ones. Why is this you say? Well, you want to avoid paying an enormous amount of accumulated interest on these credit cards.

The longer it takes for you to pay down these credit cards, the larger the amount of interest you will pay. The higher the interest rate the more you pay on your credit card balance due. So, you want to start bringing your balances down as soon as possible. The goal is to bring your credit card balances to zero. Here are a few tips you may want to consider when you try to pay off your high interest credit cards or other credit card balances:

Tip One

Start paying off your higher interest rate credit cards

first. This will help you to get on top of your finances sooner than later. In addition, this will also assist you in reducing the amount of interest that you will pay in the long run.

Tip Two

Pay more than the minimum amount due. Remember if you only pay the minimum due you'll never significantly reduce your credit card balance. This is because you are mostly paying interest due on the credit card and not to the principle amount.

Tip Three

Make your credit card payment timely. Yes that's right make sure to make your credit card payment on time. This will ensure that your payment is not received late and that you will not pay a late fee if your credit card company receives your payment on time.

By the way, if your credit card payment is not paid on time, this will usually increase the rate that you will pay on your credit card and may also affect your FICO score. So pay your credit card payment on time. It's so important and should be a primary concern for you.

Tip Four

Check your credit card account balance either online via the internet or by telephone to ensure that your payment has been applied to your account after you have made the payment. Make sure to keep track of your credit card balance. This will help to reassure you that your balance is decreasing and is a reinforcement to you that you are close to your goal of paying off your credit card balance.

Tip Five

After you have achieved your goal of paying off your credit card, do not shut down your account! This may negatively impact your FICO score by closing your account. Just hold onto your credit card and put it away. It's okay to have a credit card that is paid off with a zero balance. You may want to charge something on your credit card periodically to keep it active to possibly avoid closure of your credit card account for non usage by your creditor. Keep your charge amount to a minimum so it's easy for you to pay off the balance on your account.

Now, just think it will make you feel so good to have your credit card paid off. You will not only have the personal satisfaction that you have disciplined yourself to stay on target by paying off your credit card, but, it would also have given you an opportunity to pursue a possible long term goal of becoming debt free for the future.

Chapter 2
How Do I Keep On Track To Pay My Bills On Time?

You can stay on track to pay your bills on time by getting organized. That's right the key to staying on top of your bills is by being organized. Believe it or not being organized will usually ensure that you are able to do the following:

- Assist you with paying your bills on time.
- Avoiding late fees because you are paying your bills on time.
- Knowing your account balances.
- Track dates when your bills are paid and when your bills are received.
- Your ability to increase your FICO score by making your payments on time and decreasing the balances on your outstanding bills.
- Your ability to control your personal finances including your overall spending.

You're probably wondering at this point, how can I get organized to stay on track to keep my bills paid timely? Well, here are some tips to assist you with this:

Tip One

Create a budget. You can actually start a handwritten budget of all your monthly expenses and net income received. Or, you can use an online budget software program to assist you in creating your budget. The most important thing is to create a monthly budget which includes all of the expenses that you currently have each month and the actual net income that you receive.

Tip Two

As part of creating your monthly budget make sure to put information within your budget on when your bills are due. In addition, notate within your budget when your net income is received during the month. You will probably break up your monthly expenses and net income due in biweekly increments. That means a budget projection of your bills due around the first and the fifteenth of the month including the net income you will have to pay the bills that are due.

Tip Three

After establishing your biweekly expenses and income sheet, consider putting specific dates on this sheet for each month while you are doing your bills biweekly. If you do your bills weekly then you can use this same information on a weekly basis.

Tip Four

Keep in mind that your monthly budget may change based on certain expenses that may be paid annually or semiannually like vehicle insurance, homeowners and renters insurance. Just make sure you make the necessary adjustments needed to your budget to account for these additional expenses. You may want to also keep in mind that part of your monthly expenses should include savings and household emergency expenses as well.

Tip Five

Keep copies of your monthly budget throughout the year. Consider filing your monthly budget sheets for each year in a filing cabinet or other filing source you may choose to use. You may need this information for future reference, you never know.

Tip Six

Consider creating file folders for each creditor you have and note when your payment has been made directly on the bill. You may want to note the date and how you paid this bill either via online bill payment or a check from your account. Place this information in the creditor's file folder and put this information in a safe place.

Tip Seven

You may want to consider using your monthly budget to reconcile your bank account. This will also assist you in tracking your expenses. It is good to consider tracking your checking account balance with your budget.

See how creating a monthly budget is the key to staying on track to pay your bills on time and how important this is to you. This method will assist you in staying organized and more in control of your personal finances. So go ahead and get started on creating your monthly budget today, you'll be glad you did!

Chapter 3
Are You Scared Of Your Checkbook?

You're probably wondering how could I be scared of my checkbook? What does this really mean? Well, if you avoid posting checks, debit withdrawals or balancing your checkbook at any and all costs because other things seem more important to you, then you may have a fear of your own checkbook.

You really don't want to know what your balance is and you're scared that if you find out you'll really know how much money you actually have or don't have, yikes! You know eventually you'll need to find out your checking account balance, but you're just not there yet, and you really don't know what approach you should use to get there. You may want to consider some of these ways to get you past your fear of looking at your checkbook:

Tip One

Set aside time when you can actually review your checkbook. You'll need time alone in preferably a quiet area of your home. By setting aside time to review your check book you should be calm, relaxed and prepared to take on this task. Make sure you set aside enough time so you do not feel as though you're rushed. You may want to set aside a least one hour for this.

Nocita Carter

Tip Two

In reviewing your checkbook, make sure you take a look at all of your entries carefully first. Be sure you have all of your checks, debit card withdrawals, ATM withdrawals and deposits accounted for prior to attempting to start balancing your checkbook.

Tip Three

Get a recent copy of your bank transaction information which would include any checks that have cleared your account, debit card withdrawals, other miscellaneous withdrawals and deposits to your account and your bank statement. You should be able to secure a copy of your banking account's recent transactions via the internet if you are subscribed to your bank's online banking program if they have one. If not, you should be able to get this information from your bank directly via telephone or ATM machine. You'll want to know what posted to your account in order to be able to accurately determine your banking account balance.

Tip Four

During the time you're going through your bank transactions, make sure you mark them off in your checkbook and perhaps on a copy of the item you are trying to balance as complete and reviewed.

Tip Five

You may want to consider looking at certain spending trends while you're balancing your checkbook. As you're balancing your account you may be able to see certain trends that you may want to correct if needed.

Tip Six

Consider setting a routine schedule to balance your checkbook on a regular basis. Try to remain consistent with the time that you've scheduled to do this for yourself.

See, that wasn't hard at all! The more you balance your checkbook, the easier it will be each time you do it. You'll find that you've learned more about your spending habits and may be able to make adjustments that can save you money in the long run. So go ahead and get started, you'll be glad you did.

Chapter 4

How Do I Survive The High Cost Of Gas Hitting Me In My Wallet?

I don't know about you, but any increase in the cost of gas that we pay at the gas pump hurts me in my wallet. What's that you say? I say in my wallet and I'm sure you may be feeling this same pain as well when the price of gas goes up. I'm sure you're wondering like me if and when the price of gas will go back up and if so, how high will it go this time? Well, I think we should prepare ourselves for either way the price goes.

We can work on preparing ourselves to be in the survival mode if the gas prices start to creep back up. This time we will try to be proactive for any potential excessive increase in the gas prices. We've seen gas prices that have been as high as $5.00 a gallon. It appears that the future outlook for gas is that the prices may remain unstable and volatile. We are very much aware that the price of gas is easily manipulated by whatever is going on in the marketplace. The price of gas can easily go up and slowly come back down in these uncertain economic times.

High gas prices impact almost everything we try to do in some form. That's right, most everything we do is impacted by the high price we pay for gas. The higher gas prices eventually trickle down to cost us more in such areas as: food, clothing, airfare, utilities, entertainment, retail products and more. Just think, we are getting hit left and right with increased fees in these areas due to the high price that we pay for gas and it appears that this trend will continue for a long period of time.

What can we do to help ourselves in these hard economic times while we're trying to deal with our anxiety and sometimes anger over the high prices we pay for gas? Here are some tips that you may want to consider to help you cope. You may find that you have already started to make some of these adjustments already:

Tip One

Consider using public transportation if this is something you realistically can do. The modes of public transportation you may consider would be: bus, train and car pooling.

Tip Two

If you have a bicycle, consider using this mode of transportation for local short trips if this would be realistic of course.

Tip Three

Go to places that are necessary and actually needed. In other words, if it is something you want to do and it is not needed, don't do it! Consider letting your needs super-sede your wants to save in your wallet on gas. For example, necessary trips would be: work, school, doctor appoint-ments, etc....

Tip Four

Reduce your leisure, entertainment and travel com-muting distances. Consider doing more of these activities at home or near your home.

Tip Five

Consider purchasing a fuel efficient vehicle if this is within your budget. This will assist you in reducing the cost you are paying for your overall fuel costs. Look for vehicles that provide higher miles per gallon for the freeway and city. You may want to even consider a hybrid vehicle.

Tip Six

Slow down! Reduce your speed on the roadways you travel. This will also assist you in better fuel economy. Put less petal to the metal.

Tip Seven

Try to make your trips to the places you need to go count. Make a list beforehand of the places you need to travel and consider consolidating your trips. This means instead of making several multiple trips you combine trips by going to the places you need to go along the way and your list will assist you with this. For example, if you need to go to your local grocery store, cleaners and post office, just plan to make one trip instead of three separate trips back and forth from your home. You would take your list and stop at each place you need to along the way and strategically make sure that you plan your stops based on where these particular places are located. This really can work well if you plan your list ahead of time. Just by doing this you can save on gas.

Tip Eight

Locate and compare prices of gas stations in your area to determine who has the lowest price on fuel and consider going there for gas. A good way to do this is when you are driving to the places you need to go, just observe the gas station prices along the way and you will be able to determine which locations have the best prices for your money.

Tip Nine

Talk to your relatives, friends, neighbors, coworkers and others on the gas stations they are getting their gas from. You can compare with each other on which gas stations have the lowest prices to get your fuel. You would be helping each other this is similar to networking.

Tip Ten

Make sure your tires are property inflated. This can also assist in providing you with better fuel economy.

Tip Eleven

Count from one to ten and try to relax before you start to pump your gas to assist you in relieving your anxiety and stress over the amount of money you will be paying for the gas you are about to put into your tank.

So as a way of survival of any future gas hikes since our economy is so unpredictable, consider these tips to help you if we go back to an increased bump in prices at the pump! Just be prepared. In the short and long run we must do what we have to do to help ourselves through this major problem that is affecting our wallets. So, do what you can to help yourself and your family to reduce the amount of money you may be spending on gas.

Chapter 5
Doing Your Personal Finance Home Work, What Is This?

That means working on a consistent basis to keep your personal finance house in order. You say really, how do I go about doing this? There are many ways for you to keep your own personal finances in order. Here are some tips that may assist you on how you can go about doing this:

Tip One

Create a personal finance budget for yourself and your family. You can do this by categorizing how your money is spent such as; rental or mortgage expenses, food, entertainment, utilities, credit and debit card expenditures, savings, income, travel, etc...I think you get the idea. Just categorize your budget with what makes you comfortable. You may want to utilize a software program to assist you with the budget you create that has a spreadsheet incorporated within the program. By the way, you may also want to consider setting up your budget on a monthly basis. Your budget should assist you in determining where your money actually goes.

Tip Two

By all means get your credit report and credit score. You may want to consider running your credit report on an annual basis. Did you know that you're entitled to a free copy of your credit report from each of the credit bureaus (Equifax, TransUnion, Experian) every year? You can secure a copy of your credit report by going through www.free-annualcreditreport.com   So, go ahead and order your credit report so you can check it for accuracy. If you have any problems with your report, you'll need to contact the particular credit bureau directly. The contact information for the creditor will be provided when you've secured a copy of your credit report. By the way, you'll have to pay a few dollars extra to get your credit score separately from the credit bureaus. But, it's well worth it knowing how your credit is being scored overall.

Tip Three

Work on determining from your budget and credit report what problems you may have with your finances. These tools should assist you in what you need to do to improve or maintain your finances. It's like a snapshot of where your money is really going. So you don't have to ask the question, where did all of my money go?

Tip Four

Consider working on adding if you haven't already done so, savings to your budget. You may be saying, I barely have enough to make ends meet, how can I save money? Well, you can! Just say yes you can to yourself. A good way to start is by saving your change. That's right just start by saving your change. You will be surprised at the amount of money you can save by doing this. You can also set aside a certain amount of money on a weekly, biweekly or monthly basis that you would like to save. Make the amount of money you will save realistic so you can stick to your savings plan.

Tip Five

Set future financial projections for where you want to be with your budget in say one to five years. You may want to consider doing this to achieve your possible short and long term goals. For example, if you decide that you want to purchase a home in two to three years, a future financial budget projection may assist you in knowing how much money you need to save to achieve this goal. Or maybe you plan to retire in five years, again your future budget projection may assist you with this goal.

Tip Six

Take a closer look at your credit and debit card expenses in order to assist you in tracking how you are spending your money. This may help you determine if you're spending too much money in certain areas if you're trying to save.

Tip Seven

Check to see if your financial house is in order in reference to your insurance such as; vehicle insurance, medical insurance, rental insurance, homeowners insurance, life insurance, disability insurance etc...Make sure you have the insurance you need for yourself and your family. You may want to consider doing an annual check-up on your insurance, before the renewal due dates. This will give you the opportunity to reassess the insurance you currently have. You'll be glad that you did.

So, now you have it! That's what doing your personal finance homework means. You should be on your way to getting a handle on your personal finances if you have not already done so. You will be better prepared to manage your finances.

Chapter 6
Should I Pay Myself First?

Yes you certainly should. There are no if and or buts in response to this question. You really should pay yourself first. Remember you are the most important person to be paid. That's right! You've worked hard for your paycheck and your name is on it.

So make sure before you start paying your bills or whom ever else you're trying to pay, start with yours truly first. You say to yourself, I have lots of obligations, so I can't pay myself first. Don't say you can't just do. You're probably wondering what's the best way to do this and how much should I pay myself? You may want to consider some of these tips which may help to lead you in the direction to pay yourself first:

Tip One

Look at your paycheck, miscellaneous income check or direct deposit payroll stub for a moment. Take a deep breath and pat yourself on your back for all of your hard work to earn your paycheck. Just relax and take your paycheck all in, that's right. Take your time looking at your earnings before you start distributing your money. You'll be glad you did.

Tip Two

Make a decision before you start paying any bill on how much you will pay yourself. You're probably wondering how much you should pay yourself. It really doesn't matter as long as you pay yourself something. Just get in the habit of doing this each time you get paid. Just make sure you're realistic about the amount of money you're paying yourself and that you are comfortable with that amount. Once you start this habit you will find it may be difficult to stop.

Tip Three

You may want to consider placing a portion of the money you have paid yourself in a separate bank account or a place where you are comfortable with saving your money.

Tip Four

Paying yourself first can assist you in not only establishing or adding to your savings, but, can assist you in planning and budgeting for your future goals. For instance, if you're trying to purchase a home or take a vacation, paying yourself first may be able to assist you with this.

Tip Five

You may gain confidence and a better peace of mind by paying yourself first. This may lead to more control over your personal finances.

So go ahead and start paying yourself first this is a good thing for you to do. Just get in the habit of doing this.

You can start with your next paycheck or miscellaneous income you may receive. Go ahead deduct money for yourself and you'll be glad you got into this good habit of paying yourself first.

Chapter 7
Have You Found Yourself Tied Up In The Sub prime Housing Mess?

Interesting question and you may be wondering if the sub prime housing mess may be affecting you. It you don't understand what this means, well let me give you some information to increase your knowledge on this subject.

For the most part sub prime lending is also known as second chance or b-paper lending. Sub prime loans are loans made to consumers who do not have the best credit and would probably pay a higher interest rate due to their not so stellar credit. These types of loans are both risky to borrowers and lenders because of poor credit history, high interest rates and other financial factors. Sub prime loans are commonly utilized for home loans, car loans, credit cards and personal loans. In addition, sub prime loans typically carry higher interest rates than prime A-loans for borrowers with good credit.

Sub prime loans became more popular in the last few years due to the appreciation of homes, availability of more flexible adjustable rate mortgages and less rigid lending standards. The increase in appreciation created more equity in homes. This in turn allowed lenders to become more flexible in the loans granted to borrowers with less attractive credit via sub prime lending. It is noted that this also created relaxed standards by the lender in checking a person's credit history, income and requiring a down payment. In many instances, a consumer with poor credit was able to secure a home with no verification of income and no down payment was required.

Adjustable rate mortgages are one of the major factors involved in the sub prime mess. The adjustable rate mortgages consist of a variable rate that is linked to the current interest rates. These particular loans have been heavily used by lenders in the sub prime market as alternatives to fixed rate mortgages. Lenders offered low introductory adjustable rates to attract more borrowers. By doing this, many people purchased homes with these types of loans.

You're probably wondering, what happened to make borrowers end up not being able to make their mortgage payments? Well, what happened is that the federal funds rate went from one percent in 2003 and was dramatically increased to 5.5 percent. This increase in the funds interest rate was significant for the sub prime housing problem because over a three year period it left many borrowers with mortgage payments that increased dramatically.

This has created major problems for borrowers being able to continue making their mortgage payments. Some borrowers' mortgage payments have increased as much as fifty percent or more from their initial mortgage payment.

The reduction of the federal funds rate may help some borrowers with the amount they will pay for their adjustable rate mortgages.

A significant problem with the interest only or adjustable rate mortgage loans that homeowners are currently facing in unison with their high mortgage payments is the fact that most lenders are not willing to work out an arrangement or compromise with the borrower to reduce their payment. It is noted that most of the adjustable rate mortgage and interest only loans were packaged and sold as a security for investors. The packaged mortgage loan security usually contains a clause restricting working out a compromise arrangement with the borrower. Hence the majority of adjustable rate mortgages and no interest loans renewed in late 2007 and also began renewing in 2008 resulting in numerous foreclosures for homeowners. This problem continues to be an ongoing trickling down affect for homeowners.

So does all or some of this information affect you? If it does, you may want to consider contacting your lender or mortgage loan servicer to see if they would be willing to assist you with reducing your mortgage payment by getting you into a fixed rate mortgage loan you can afford. You can also contact Hope Now which is an alliance of mortgage counselors, servicers, investors and other market participants.

Hope Now is an organization that reaches out to homeowners who are facing foreclosure and who need assistance in trying to remain in their homes. To obtain information concerning approved mortgage counselors or to discuss your particular mortgage problem, you may want to consider contacting the Hope Now hotline at 1-888-995-HOPE or 888-995-4673.

Chapter 8
Do You Know What's Going On With Your Pension Plan?

That's a good question, do you know whether or not your pension plan is stable, and if so will it remain that way? Well, if you're part of your employer's pension plan, you should find out the answers to these questions. Once you find out, stay informed about your pension plan. It is also important to know whether or not your employer even offers a pension plan. Not all companies offer pensions to their employees.

You say you know you have a pension plan but really don't know what this is. A pension plan is a retirement account that your employer contributes funds as part of your future retirement. The amount paid to your retirement fund by your employer is based on the number of years you have worked and the amount of income you have earned. In addition, your pension will be determined based on whether or not you are qualified for the plan based the number of years your employer requires you to be vested with their company. Vesting means to bestow upon someone or the person is entitled to something. In this particular case, it would be a pension plan if the employee is fully

Nocita Carter

vested as an employee of a particular company that offers such a plan.

How long will it take for me to become eligible for my employer's pension plan? It is normally between three to five years when you become eligible for the plan offered by your employer.

What if I no longer work for the employer after I become eligible will I still be vested? Yes.

I hear some employers have terminated their pension plans, why is this? Some employers are finding it very expensive to continue with their pension plans due to the increased number of retirees, low interest rates and instability of the stock market.

My employer is terminating our pension plan, how will this affect me? The government agency Pension Benefit Guaranty Corporation will pick up pension payments when the employer defaults. Note, this agency pays a certain amount of your pension benefits on an annual basis. Unfortunately in most cases you will receive less for your annual pension amount then you would normally have received via your employer.

Is there any way to know if my employer's pension plan is in trouble? If your company is showing signs of financial trouble, normally the first thing to go is the pension plan. If you are trying to find out if your employer may be headed for financial trouble consider checking the following: financial news information on your company, newspaper financial section, stock market, business financial magazines and the internet.

I just recently found out that an employer I worked for a few years ago just went out of business. How would I find out about the status of my pension plan that I had with this employer, I've been unable to contact them directly? If your past or former employer defaulted on it's pension plan, check the Pension Benefit Guaranty Corporation website at www.pbgc.gov to see if this program has taken over the handling of your former employer's plan.

Stay on top of your pension plan, by keeping yourself informed of your plan's current status. This is important because your pension is part of your retirement for your future. If you don't stay informed about your pension, you may loose valuable funds that are important for your future retirement needs.

Chapter 9

Looking For A Way To Get Yourself Established and You Do Not Have Any Credit?

You can start working on getting your credit established by considering a few methods that may help you to get on track. You may want to consider getting an unsecured credit card to start establishing your credit history.

You're probably wondering what is a secured credit card? It means putting up your own money as collateral for a particular credit card account as security. This money is used as the amount you would charge against your credit card limit for your account. You would make a payment each month on this account which would establish a payment history for you. Get the picture? You're establishing your credit with your own money as collateral for the secured credit card.

You can check various websites such as; www.credit.com to apply for a secured credit card. Typically, when you have a secured credit card, the monies that you deposit into your account are equal to your credit limit. The interest rates charged for the secured credit cards are typically higher than the prevailing credit card interest rates. In addition, there is usually an annual fee. However, once you have established a good payment history with the secured credit card for approximately one year, you may be able to apply for an unsecured credit card with a lower interest rate with better terms and conditions.

A company named Payment Reporting Builds Credit(www.prbc.com) specializes in securing data on rent and other recurring payments. A consumer can enter their information into a web file and they are charged by PRBC a fee to verify, or set-up an automatic bill pay via your bank and have the records sent to Payment Reporting Builds Credit(PRBC).

PRBC also reports information on rents paid for apartments from data secured from www.rentbureau.com. Rent Bureau collects rental histories on various apartment units.

By utilizing some or all of these methods you should be well on your way to getting your credit established. Just be persistent in the payment methods that you are utilizing for the program you have chosen to get your credit on track. Stay focused and you will probably be in a position to go from the nontraditional method of establishing your credit with secured credit cards to establishing or even reestablishing your credit with unsecured cards.

Chapter 10

Ready For Your Credit To Get Tightened Up? If Not, Change Is Here Ready Or Not!

That's right! Right now we are facing a record level of homes in foreclosure, declining home values, increased unemployment, increased interest rates on credit cards, and more scrutinizing of loan applications by lenders. Heck, you may already be facing these problems right now.

Home values in certain parts of the United States continue to decline. The sub prime mess has created a record number of home owners who are unable to make their loan payments. This is due to the acceleration of their loan payment based on their adjustable interest rates changing the amount of payment they would be making on their loan. In many cases this leaves the homeowner with the inability to make their payment placing them in a financial bind.

It's gotten so bad that some lenders with the urging of our government are trying to assist some homeowners in negotiating a better loan payment to make their payment more affordable. Some homeowners may qualify for these particular programs provided by lenders. However, some homeowners will not qualify for these programs leaving them in a financial bind and with the possibility of losing their home.

Did you know that in the midst of the problems we are currently having, if you have a home equity line of credit you may be stopped from using your line of credit by your lender? That's right, the line of credit you have may not be available to you. Some lenders have tightened up credit so much that they have decided for some homeowners they will either hold, suspend or reduce their line of credit. So if you have a home equity line of credit you may want to take a look at following up with your lender if you are concerned whether or not this will affect you.

Have you noticed whether or not the interest rates for your credit cards have increased? If your interest rate has changed you may want to contact your credit card company to find out why your interest rate has increased. If your rate has been increased by your credit card company, see if you can get the company to reduce your rate. Just keep in mind that you may be more successful in doing this if you make your payments timely and you maintain good credit.

It is also important to ensure that you pay all of your bills on time. In some instances, your interest rate for your credit cards may increase if you do not pay your other bills on time. Beware, your creditors are looking at this as well.

If you have been paying your bills on time and maintain good credit and your lender refuses to reduce your interest rate, you may want to consider checking other credit card companies interest rates. If you can find a lower rate you may want to consider going with the lower interest rate for that particular credit card company.

Overall, just beware that times are tougher out there and your credit is being looked at more and more by your lenders. Just stay on top of your credit by paying your bills on time, securing all of your credit reports from the three credit bureaus annually, and communicate with your lender if you are having problems making your payments or need their assistance.

Chapter 11
Identity Theft, What Is This And How Do I Protect Myself?

Identity Theft is when someone uses another person's social security number, driver license, name, address, telephone number and any other information about that particular person as their own. The unauthorized person that obtains this information without the other person's knowledge uses this information to commit theft and fraud.

How does a person committing identity theft get my information? By going through your trash, hacking into a computer that you may use, securing a copy of your credit report, stealing credit card and debit card numbers that you may have, stealing your mail, completing a change of address form to reroute your mail to a different address, stealing your purse or wallet, and scamming information from you by posing as a business person.

How would I know if I am a victim of identity theft? If you receive credit card statements for accounts you did not apply for, you do not receive your mail, your credit is being denied and you do not know why, counterfeit checks are used to withdraw money from your bank account, you receive calls from collection agencies about bills for accounts established with your personal information that you do not know about, and other problems that you may have with your personal information.

Should I order a copy of my credit reports to find out if I am a victim of identity theft? Yes, you may want to consider doing this if you suspect that you are a victim of identity theft. You would want to order a copy of your credit reports from all three credit reporting agencies which are: Equifax www.equifax.com 1-800-685-1111; Experian www.experian.com 1-888-397-3742; and; TransUnion www.transunion.com 1-800-916-8800.

What should I do if my identity is stolen by someone? Contact the three credit reporting agencies as soon as possible and let them know that you are a victim of identity theft and ask them to place a fraud alert on your statement as a victim in your credit report file. Order a copy of your credit report from each agency to check the information on your report. Contact the credit reporting agencies fraud units at these telephone numbers or addresses: Equifax: 1-800-525-6285, P.O. Box 74021, Atlanta, GA. 30374-0241: Experian: 1-888-397-3742, P.O. Box 9532, Allen, TX. 75013:: TransUnion: 1-800-680-7289, Fraud Victim Assistance Division, P.O. Box 6790, Fullerton, CA. 92834-6790.

Should I close my credit and checking accounts if identity theft has occurred? Yes, you may want to consider closing your credit and checking accounts if you suspect identity theft. Contact your bank and creditors about your identity being stolen and consider closing your accounts and establish new ones. If your checks are stolen, request that your bank notify the check verification company that they use.

You may also want to contact the major check verification companies as well.

The major check verification companies that you would want to contact are the following: TeleCheck, 1800-366-2425 and Certegy Inc., 1-800-437-5120. You may also want to contact a company known as Scan at 1-800-262-7771 to find out if an identity thief has been using your checks. In addition, you should also contact your local police department and report that your identity has been stolen. Make sure that you file a complaint with the Federal Trade Commission about your identity being stolen as well. You can file this report at www.consumer.gov/idtheft.

Chapter 12
How Often Should I Check My Credit Report?

You may want to consider checking what's on your credit report at least once a year. That's right at least once a year get a copy of all three of your credit reports. You will want to know what each credit bureau (TransUnion, Experian and Equifax) has listed on your reports. You don't want any surprises when you apply for credit or seek new employment.

So, as a general rule it's a good idea to get copies of your credit reports at least once a year. You will also be able to find out whether or not someone has ordered credit in your name without your authorization. Here are some tips and information which may assist you in your quest to get your credit reports:

Tip One

How do I go about contacting the credit report bureaus? You contact the bureaus either in writing or via the internet with the following information: TransUnion, P.O. Box 2000, Chester, PA. 19022, 800-888-4213, www.transunion.com; Equifax, P.O. Box 740256, Atlanta, GA. 30374, 877-784-2528www.equifax.com; Experian, P.O. Box 2104, Allen, TX. 75013, 888-397-3742 , www.experian.com.

Tip Two

Can I get a free copy of my credit report? Yes you can receive a copy of your free credit report on an annual basis at no cost from www.freeannualcreditreport.com. You can also secure free copies of your credit reports directly from each credit bureau.

Tip Three

Should I get a copy of my FICO score? Yes, this would be a good idea to find out where you stand in reference to your credit score. As you may be aware, your credit score is used in determining whether or not you will qualify for credit you have applied for and the interest rate you will receive. The higher your credit scores the better chances you have of getting a lower interest rate and approval of your credit. In addition, FICO scores are now being used by many employers during the pre-employment process.

Tip Four

How can I improve my credit and credit score? By paying your bills on time and paying your credit card balance in full if at all possible. Make sure you stay current with paying your bills. This will assist you in improving your credit overall.

Tip Five

If there is an error on my credit report, how do I

go about fixing the problem? Contact the credit bureau directly concerning the error on your report in writing and request that the error be corrected. You may want to also contact the creditor directly that is reporting the negative information listed on your report and get them to correct the error. You will also want the creditor to provide you with a written confirmation of them correcting the error to your credit report. The credit bureau has thirty days to respond to your request about erroneous information listed on your credit report.

Tip Six

Should I consider hiring a credit repair company to fix my credit? No. This is not a good idea! The only one able to fix your credit problem is you. Some credit repair agencies charge several hundred dollars in fees claiming they can repair your credit. Some of these agencies even offer you a new social security number to establish new credit. This is absolutely illegal, you do not want to be a party to this scam at all. It's best that you fix your own credit the right way by doing the following: contact the credit bureaus about any errors or discrepancies you have on your credit report; contact the creditor directly about errors listed by them on your report; pay your bills on time; and, try to pay off your credit balances as soon as you can.

Ordering a copy of your credit reports is a good idea. The sooner you start this annual practice of getting your credit report the better off you will be. This will give you a better peace of mind and will hopefully eliminate surprises when you go to apply for employment and future credit for the purchase of a home, vehicle, or whatever else you would like to purchase.

Chapter 13
Is Your Out Of Control Spending Eating Your Money?

Are you getting past due notices on bills you thought you paid? Did you try to take money out of your bank account and you found out your account's overdrawn? Or, did you try to pay for your groceries and found out that your check, debit card or credit card was rejected and you can't pay for the groceries you need to feed your family? Or maybe, you went to your favorite retail store to purchase an item you thought you could not live without and attempted to charge it to your credit card and you were told your purchase is declined. You probably have a symptom that involves a spending habit which is out of control. You're trying to figure out what should I do to control my spending? Here are some tips you may want to consider which include the following:

Tip One

Get a copy of your bank statement to find out about the items which have gone through your account which include: checks, debits, deposits and withdrawals. This will help you to find out where you are in your spending. You've gotta start somewhere, so this is a good place to begin.

Tip Two

Work on reducing your spending. What do I mean by this? Well, cut out items you want but really don't need. For instance, consider reducing your shopping if you find yourself in stores on a daily or weekly basis. Just by reducing your shopping you can save yourself lots of money.

Tip Three

Consider reducing your entertainment expenses by going out less. Reducing entertainment such as movies, restaurants, coffee houses, concerts, etc..., will save you money in your wallet. It may be tough to do at first, but, you'll like it in the end because your money will begin to grow.

Tip Four

Write down what you spend in order to keep track of your money. This will enable you to determine where you are spending your money. You will be able to make adjustments easily if you need to.

Tip Five

You may want to even consider keeping a weekly or monthly savings log which will give you an idea of the amount of money you are actually saving when you have reduced your expenditures. You will be able to create this log based on you keeping track of the money you are spending. This will reinforce the effort you have made to reduce your spending my giving you information on the amount of money you are actually keeping in your bank account. Indeed this is positive feedback for you to keep striving to keep your expenditures down and in check.

See you really can work on your spending to keep your money from being eaten if you set your mind to it. You've just got to start working on it and you should be able to accomplish your goal of gaining control over your personal finances. It just takes work, but you can do it just get started now!

Chapter 14
How Soon Should I Teach My Kid To Save?

It's never too soon to teach your kids how to save. In fact, the sooner you teach them how to save the better they will be at learning how to manage their money in the future. If they start early saving, they will understand the value of money and how much can be accumulated over time by saving. How should I start teaching my child how to save? A good way to start is to follow some of these tips to assist you with helping your child to save:

Tip One

Give your child an allowance which will provide your child with money that they can manage. Encourage your child to save a least half of their allowance.

Tip Two

Show your kid how much interest they can earn over time on their money when they save it. Especially the power of compound interest.

Tip Three

By saving money today your kids would have money saved for a future purchase they may want to make.

Nocita Carter

Tip Four

Make saving fun for your child. Have your child put their savings in a piggy bank or jar so they can watch their money grow.

Tip Five

Open a bank account for your child and let them deposit money from their allowance or other monies received into their bank account.

You say this is all good information, however, you're unable to give your child an allowance because you just don't have the money. What should I do, I really want my child to learn how to save? Don't fret, they can still save money. You can teach your child how to save by collecting bottles and cans to earn money so they can start saving. No matter how much money your child may earn every amount of money they save adds up. So, it seems easy, it really is. Get your child into the habit of saving today, so they will start learning how to manage their personal finances now and for the future.

Chapter 15
Should I Get Financing Before I Make A Major Purchase?

Yes, yes and yes! Get your financing before you start shopping for a home, vehicle or other major purchase. By doing this beforehand you'll save yourself lots of money. Not only that, you'll be in a great position to negotiate your purchase with the seller. There are so many ways that you can shop for your financing these days. Here are some tips and information to assist you with finding out where you can start looking for your financing needs:

Tip One

Using the internet is a great way to do research on your financing. The internet provides you with an array of financing options to choose from. You get to check on what company provides you with the best interest rate for your needs. You'll even find financing options you didn't even realize are available to you.

Tip Two

Your own bank. Go to your bank and apply for the

financing you need. Get pre approved for your loan prior to making your purchase. What better place to secure your financing than your own bank. You're banking with them so why not consider giving them the opportunity to help you with your major purchase. Just make sure the interest rate their charging you is a good one.

Tip Three

Consider credit union financing. Sometimes you'll find lower interest rates for that major purchase you're trying to make via a credit union. Credit unions are also competing for your business as well and have become major players in the financial world these days. This is good, because you have another outlet to secure your financing from. There are some instances that you will be able to qualify for membership at various credit unions. So make sure you check into this.

Tip Four

Check your local newspaper, phone book and other media sources for prospective companies that provide financing that you may consider using.

Tip Five

As a last resort, consider using the seller's financing provided. The seller may have competitive interest rates you may be interested in applying for to make the major purchase you're interested in. Just make sure the interest rate is truly low for your needs and the best rate that you can qualify for.

So as you can see, there are several financing options available to you to secure your financing before you make your major purchase. You'll have the edge on your seller when you're getting ready to make your purchase. Yes that's right! You can negotiate how much you're paying for that home, vehicle or other major purchase before you sign on the dotted line. You're in the driver's seat because you have your money already, remember you're already pre approved. So let the negotiations for your major purchase begin. Make sure you stay in control and pay the best interest rate that you can for your next major purchase. You'll be happy you took the time to get preapproved for your loan.

Chapter 16

Should I Save My Mad Money For A Rainy Day?

Yes, this is a good idea. I know you want to know what is mad money? Well, an example of what this term means is when a young lady went out with her friend to a party and her friend left her at the party with no way home. She became mad with her friend that left her at the party and luckily for her, she had money stowed away in her shoe to take a cab back home. She thought to herself on her way home in the cab, that it was good that her mother had taught her to always have money set aside for emergency situations such as this.

Thank goodness, this young lady had the forethought to stash her mad money away so she could take a cab back home, since her friend left her in a lurch. Get the point? Having an emergency fund whether it is mad money or saved money, is important for you to have. You say, how do I go about doing this? Well, you can read these tips to help you learn what you can do:

Tip One

Set up a savings account specifically for your emergency fund or mad money fund. Whatever you want to call it, just establish one.

Tip Two

Deposit a certain amount of money on a weekly, biweekly, or monthly basis in your account. You may want to set up automatic deposits to your account via your payroll department. Or, you may want to have your bank automatically withdraw a certain amount of money from your checking account into your emergency or mad money savings account.

Tip Three

Try to save at least six months of your monthly salary to cover your bills if you were to loose your job. This amount of time will hopefully allow you the cushion you will need until you secure new employment.

Tip Four

The money you save in your emergency or mad money account should be used for household emergencies, personal emergencies or if you're no longer able to work. Don't use it for other expenditures such as bills, travel, etc...Get the idea? It's a savings account that you don't want to touch unless it's absolutely necessary.

Tip Five

Make sure the bank account you put your emergency or mad money into, is paying you the most interest you can earn for this account. Research as many sources as possible on securing the best interest rate you can get. Check with your bank, the internet, newspaper and other sources for the prevailing interest rate. You want to make sure your money can be accessed easily and quickly if you need it for an emergency.

By establishing an emergency or mad money fund, this will give you a better peace of mind if you need access to money when there is an emergency in your life. So, the sooner you start setting money aside for a rainy day, the better off you will be.

Make sure the amount of money you contribute to your emergency or mad money fund is realistic for your budget. Save as much as you can without upsetting your overall personal or family finances. So go ahead and get started today.

Chapter 17
Want To Loose Your Debt?

I'm sure your answer is yes to this question. Yeah, you may want to loose your debt, but aren't sure exactly how to do this. Did you know that there are a lot of people in the United States who are in more debt today than we've ever been? We are also saving much less. That's right, even though we make more money we're saving a lot less than our grandparents did. I know you're saying things cost much more these days. Yes, I know, but we're still spending more, which keeps us from saving the money we should for a rainy day.

In fact, the interest rates that are currently being charged on credit cards average eighteen percent and upward. Ouch! That's a lot of interest to pay for a credit card especially if you don't pay off your balance each month. Of course, your credit card company would like you to keep a balance on your credit card so they can collect interest from you. Remember you're charged interest on your unpaid balance, that's how the credit card companies are able to make enormous amounts of money.

You say to yourself, what can I do to reduce or eliminate my debt? Well, here are some tips to help you begin your path to financial freedom by reducing and eventually eliminating your debt:

Tip One

Review all of your current billing statements to determine how much you owe your creditors. By doing this, you'll know exactly where you stand with your bills and exactly how much you owe.

Tip Two

Look at the highest interest rates you are paying and the balances of these particular credit cards. Based on those balances, attempt to start paying off the credit cards with the highest interest rates first. This will assist you in reducing the amount of interest you are paying to your creditors sooner.

Tip Three

Pay more than the minimum amount due on your credit cards. You want to get your debt reduced and eventually eliminated by paying over the minimum balance that the credit card company is requiring you to pay. Remember debt elimination is your goal, so this will help you to work towards that.

Tip Four

Make sure to pay your bills on time in order to avoid late fees and extra interest charges added to your credit balances. You definitely don't want to pay your credit card company any more money than needed. Remember, the more money you keep for yourself, the more you have to save.

Tip Five

Try to keep spending on your credit cards to a minimum. That's right, you're trying to become debt free, so you'll need to eliminate or reduce your spending on your credit cards. Yes, I know you'll need a credit card for emergencies or certain needed expenditures just try to use your credit card with caution. Your goal is to stay out of debt and to become debt free.

Tip Six

You may want to take money from your savings or money market account to pay off your credit cards so you can become debt free or reduce your debt. If you decide to do this, make sure you keep some money in your savings for an emergency or a rainy day.

Tip Seven

If you think you need debt counseling, then you may want to seek professional help to assist you with reducing or eliminating your debt. Just do some research via the internet or other sources to locate a company that specializes in debt counseling. Just make sure the organization you choose is legitimate.

These tips should help you get started on your way to becoming debt free for the future. You'll be glad that you decided to take this crucial step in taking control of your personal finances by losing your debt. Remember, it's important for your future.

Chapter 18
What Should I Do If I Want To Catch Up On My Retirement Planning?

Good question and even better you're thinking in the right direction about your future which is someday retiring. If you're one of those people who haven't saved any or very much money for your retirement, it's never too late for you to start now! It's important that you do start and soon.

It doesn't take long for age to slip up on you fast if you know what I mean. So, just get started on your retirement planning now while you're thinking about it. You may want to consider some of these tips and information to get you started:

Tip One

If the employer you are working for offers a 401K plan wherein you contribute a percentage of your earnings towards retirement, consider signing up for this plan. In most instances, the employer may match a percentage of the contributions you make to your 401K account. Your contributions can be made on a pre-tax or after tax basis which will help your money grow in your account.

Tip Two

You may want to consider taking a second job to add more income for your retirement. This will assist you in increasing the amount of money for your retirement fund. If you're able to fit a second job into your schedule, make sure this would be feasible for you and your family without causing problems.

Tip Three

Save more of your money by cutting back on some of your expenses. You may want to reduce the number of times you eat out, go to the movies, shop, and any other areas you can cut back on to save towards your retirement.

Tip Four

Consider saving your change! That's right, save your change. You would be surprised at the amount of money you can accumulate in a small amount of time by saving your change. Your change could be set aside for your retirement fund. So, start putting your coins away for your future.

Tip Five

Reduce or eliminate your spending on your credit cards. The less you pay on your credit cards, the more money you'll have to save towards your retirement. So, if you can pay cash for that item you need to purchase, do that instead of charging it to your credit card. You'll not only save yourself interest charges, but, you'll have extra money to put away for your retirement.

Tip Six

If you have a home and are using it as a cash machine or atm by taking out your home equity via loans or a credit line, stop what you're doing! Your home is one of your largest investments and will most likely be a retirement vehicle for you. You'll either want to have your home paid off prior to retirement or be in a position to sell your home to obtain the equity to use as retirement income. If you have your home equity tapped out, then you will not be in the position during your golden years to enjoy your retirement. You'll probably be still paying a mortgage that you may not be able to afford and will not have much money in your retirement fund.

It's better late than never when it comes to starting your retirement planning. So, go ahead, start working on catching up with your retirement planning today, you'll be glad you did.

Chapter 19
My Adult Child Wants To Move Back In With Me, Should I Let My Child Do This?

Well, that's a good question and continues to be a dilemma for most parents. As a parent you want to help your adult child, but you want your child to become independent of you in most cases. You want your adult child to spread their wings and find their own space. But, sometimes that may be more difficult in our present day due to the high cost of housing.

It may take your adult child more time to save up for their first apartment or home. Especially if they just finished college and may have student loans that they will need to pay back. So, you really want to help your adult child by letting them live with you, but, you want them not to become dependant upon you if you help them. Here are some tips and information you may want to consider when thinking about letting your adult child live with you:

Tip One

Consider charging your adult child rent while they are

staying with you once they have secured a job. This will teach your adult child responsibility and how to manage their personal finances. They'll need this experience in the future when they have their own apartment or home.

Tip Two

If you don't want to charge your adult child rent or don't believe their financially able to pay rent, consider having them pay part or all of a utility bill which would include the electric, gas or cable bill.

Tip Three

If your adult child wants to use your telephone, make sure they have their own telephone line or cell phone wherein they are responsible for paying their own bill. This will eliminate future headaches for you later, if your phone bill increases to an astronomical amount, due to your adult child living in your home.

Tip Four

Consider having your adult child purchase their own food or contribute to the purchase. You may find that your food bill may increase substantially when your adult child moves in. So, in order to alleviate problems with the potential added cost, have your adult child contribute to the cost or get their own food. Remember you're trying to teach them responsibility and how to manage their own personal finances. So this is a way to do this.

Tip Five

Set ground rules for your adult child prior to them

moving into your home. Remember, the bottom line is, this is your home and you want to be comfortable while your adult child is living with you. Make sure you make it clear whether or not your adult child can have a boyfriend or girlfriend stay overnight in your home, responsibility for certain household chores and any additional ground rules you may want to discuss with your adult child. This will hopefully alleviate problems in the future.

Tip Six

You may want to consider setting a time frame for how long your adult child can live with you. That is if you want them to eventually get out on their own and become self sufficient. By doing this, your adult child will continue to learn responsibility and full independence by getting a place of their own.

It's okay to help your adult child by letting them live with you. However, you don't want them to be dependant on you forever. You want them to be financially secure to become self sufficient and independent which would enable them to take care of themselves in their own place. After all, you've raised them to carry their own torch so they can be prepared when you're no longer able to assist them.

Chapter 20

If I Receive A Lay Off Notice From My Job What Should I Do?

Try not to panic if this happens to you first and foremost! Unfortunately, in these economic times the number of people facing this dilemma of becoming unemployed is continuing to grow significantly. This seems to be the current climate due to the condition of our economy.

We are seeing record numbers of individuals in both blue collar and white collar jobs heading for the unemployment lines. You ask what should you do if you anticipate being laid off or maybe you have received your notice of termination from your employer? You may want to consider some of these tips before you leave your employer:

Tip One

Secure information concerning your health insurance from your employer. You will want to know how long your current health care benefits will last and when will your COBRA start. COBRA also known as Consolidated Omnibus Budget Reconciliation Act, is a continuation of your health care benefits at your expense for a certain period

Nocita Carter

of time and is usually temporary health coverage. Make sure to take the time to discuss this information with your employer. It is very important that you take the time to do this.

Tip Two

Find out information concerning your pension plan if this benefit is available through your employer. Get the facts on whether or not you are eligible for the pension plan and if so how would this work for you. Secure documentation concerning your pension benefits. It does not matter if you would be able to tap into your pension benefits at the time of your termination from your employer if you are already vested or eligible for the plan. It's just important that you have literature or documentation that provides

you with written detail concerning the pension benefits you may qualify for as an employee.

Tip Three

Secure information on your 401K plan or other employee retirement plan information your company provides if you believe you may be eligible. You will want to also obtain documentation or literature concerning this plan information for your records.

Tip Four

Attempt to negotiate with your employer disability and life insurance benefits you currently have. Disability and life insurance is important and in some instances for many people is difficult to secure. It may be easier to negotiate with your employer to keep these benefits and pay if possible, at your employer's group rate which is normally discounted. It is usually more expensive to secure disability and life insurance on your own after you leave your employer. Keep in mind that in most cases, you are now older since arriving at your current employer and your health may have changed as well. As you continue to age, your life insurance and disability insurance increases over time as well.

Tip Five

You will also want to find out how much vacation time you have with your employer. If there are any discrepancies concerning your vacation time available, you will be able to secure clarification of this information before you depart from your employer.

Tip Six

Secure information on unemployment benefits that may be available to you. You will want to discuss this information with your employer and your local unemployment office. This will assist you in knowing the amount of money you will receive while you
are unemployed and for how long you will be eligible for this benefit. In addition, you may want to find out if there is unemployment extensions granted if you are not able to secure employment within six months after being laid off.

Tip Seven

It is difficult when you have been laid off from your

job. So, try to relax take a deep breath, regroup and think about how you plan on taking your next step in how you will survive being temporarily unemployed. Just keep in mind with persistence, patience, diligence and determination you will be well on your way to making it through this temporary setback.

The majority of employees do not want to be laid off from their place of employment. However, you want to prepare yourself for what you will need financially to sustain yourself and your family while you are unemployed. Make sure to secure the information you need from your employer before you are laid off. It is also important to ask questions and secure answers from your employer on information that you need before you leave your employer. Take the proactive approach and refuse to be reactive to getting the information you need, insist on it!

Chapter 21
Save Money By Saving Your Change!

Save money by saving your change can add up to thousands of dollars for your nest egg! That's right, by taking the change you have in your pockets, purse, vehicle or anywhere you keep change, can help you to start saving money. Think about it, you can start saving your change today and you are guaranteed if you continue to save your change every day, that you will save a significant amount of money over time.

You've been saying that it's hard for you to save, and you just don't make enough money to be able to do this. Well, you can start slow by just taking that spare change you have lying around and putting it in a jar and just let it grow over time. It won't take long before your change jar starts growing and you now have money saved.

Imagine when you count the amount of change you've saved, after six months of dropping your change in your jar, you are astounded at how much money you have collected in just a short period of time. You can do it, just start saving your change today! Don't wait to save, it doesn't matter that you're starting out small by saving your change. It only matters that you just start saving. These tips may help you when you start saving your change:

Nocita Carter

Tip One

Get yourself a jar, piggy bank or some type of container to put your change in. Nothing fancy is needed, the idea is get yourself something that you can use to start saving your change.

Tip Two

Make it a goal to collect all your change and put it in a jar on a daily basis from your purse, wallet, clothing, vehicle or any other place you may have your change.

Tip Three

Put your change jar in a special place in your home where it is not tempting for you or anyone else in your home to remove change from your savings jar.

Tip Four

Make it habit to keep all the change you receive when making purchases so you can place this change in your change jar as well.

Tip Five

Plan to count your change every six months and deposit your change into a special savings account at your bank. This will assist you in keeping track on how well you're saving money by saving your change.

You may think this idea of saving money by saving your change may not work. I'm here to tell you that it will. Over the years I have used this method to save money and it has worked very well for me. In fact, I have several change jars around my home that I always use for my change. I have been able to save lots of money by doing this. It is easy and I have trained myself just to drop my change into my jars, which helps me to continuing saving money on an ongoing basis. So, if I can do it I know you can! Save money by saving your change today, so you can help yourself to improve your finances today and for your future.

Chapter 22

Comparison Shop On The Internet Before You Make Your Next Retail Store Purchase!

That's right compare prices on the internet for the product you plan to purchase you'll be glad you did. Did you know that you can literally compare the prices of the majority of the products you are interested in purchasing via the internet? Yes you can! Did you also know by doing this you may be able to save money for the product you plan to purchase and even over time the more products you are able to purchase this way could save you hundreds if not thousands of dollars in the long run.

Not only do you save money on the product you plan to purchase, but, by using the internet to comparison shop, this also allows you some time to think about whether or not you really need or want the product you are about to purchase. In a sense this slows you down so you have the opportunity to make a sound decision on your product choice. Just think this gives you the opportunity to really think about what you want to purchase and be able to make an informed decision about the product. You may want to consider these tips:

Tip One

What information do I need to comparison shop on the internet? Well, a good way to start this is by actually seeing the product you want to purchase in a retail store. Why should I do this? You will want to test the product you are considering to purchase to see if it is the product for you and if you really like your product choice. You are also able to obtain the product price, ability to see the product and determine whether or not the product you plan to purchase is user friendly and if you are comfortable with your product choice.

Make sure while you are in the retail store that you write down the exact name of the product, features information, color, model number and any other product information that you think may be useful to you when you later comparison shop your product choice via the internet.

Tip Two

After I secure the information that I need to comparison shop on the internet what do I do with this information? You take the information you have gathered about your product choice and obtain access to the internet via your home or public computer. After you have gained access to the internet then you will want to begin your product comparison shopping via the internet by utilizing a search engine such as; MSN, Google, Yahoo, etc…to look up your product to see where you may be able to purchase the item. Just type your product name into the search engine and you will find in most cases that numerous websites will come up during your search to point you to websites that sell the product you are looking for.

Consider checking several websites to comparison shop your product for the best price, free delivery or minimal delivery cost, return policy, method of payment and secured website ordering.

You will be glad that you decided to take the time to comparison shop on the internet for the product that you want. In most cases you probably ended up saving yourself money and that's a good thing. In our technological age the internet has become more and more important to us every single day. You can virtually find almost anything you want and need via the internet and have the product delivered to your door with literally the touch of your fingertips on your computer. Amazing! So, you see it's not hard to take the time to comparison shop on the internet to save you money. Just take the time to do it, and you will be happy you did.

Chapter 23

We're Getting Married Soon, Should We Talk About Our Finances?

So you plan on getting married soon, and there's just something that you've had on your mind, but you just don't know what you should do or how you should say it. That would be the questions you have concerning your future spouse's finances. You really need to know something about the finances before you say I do. You really don't know how your future spouse has paid their bills and you just need to know now before it becomes a problem later on.

Well, as the old saying goes you can't live on love, you need money to survive. Finance questions before marriage will help you and your future spouse understand where you both are financially before marriage. If your future spouse is not able to contribute financially, you will know this before you say your vows. That is why finance questions before marriage is so important. You may want to consider some or all of the following questions prior to saying I do to your future spouse:

1. How much money do you earn?
2. Can I see a copy of your credit report and FICO score?

3. Do you pay your bills on time?
4. What is the balance on your accounts for your outstanding bills?
5. Have you ever filed for bankruptcy and do you have any judgments against you?
6. Do you pay child support?
7. Do you have a savings account, insurance, investments and a retirement plan?
8. Once we get married, will we both be able to spend freely?
9. If we purchase a home will we own the home jointly?
10. Should we have a prenuptial agreement since we may own property or other assets?

Discussing your finances before marriage is important for future spouses who are planning to get married. It is a difficult subject for couples to discuss, however it is crucial in maintaining a good relationship. It may be beneficial to you and your future spouse to discuss your finances before saying your vows.

It's a good idea that you both are on the same page about how your finances are before the marriage and what your future goals will be for your finances. This may assist you both in getting past one of your most important hurdles for marriage. Discussing your finances prior to marriage may assist you and your future spouse with keeping you both on track and in a positive direction for your future goals.

Personal finances are one of the most critical key components of a marriage. In many instances, marriages have dissolved due to the fact that couples have not discussed their finances prior to the marriage taking place. Try to make sure you find out about your future spouse's finances before you get married so this does not become a problem for you later on.

Chapter 24
The Balancing Act, What Is This?

You're probably wondering what is the balancing act? Well, this is your ability to pay your credit cards, mortgage, rent, vehicle payment and any other bills on a timely basis. You attempt and hopefully succeed in paying your bills timely in order to avoid being penalized by your creditor. Did you know in today's economic times even if you pay your bills on time and have stellar credit you still may be subjected to having the interest rates on your credit cards increased, credit card limit or your home equity line of credit decreased or even closed? This could even be done by your creditor without your knowledge.

In an uncertain economy who knows what will continue to occur. What we do know is that as consumers the best thing that we can do is to try to stay ahead by paying our bills on time. It is important that we all know that the credit environment that we previously knew not so long ago is now going through a transitional phase. We must wither this storm by trying to stay on track by keeping abreast of our own credit situation. These tips may assist you in attempting to keep a balance with your own personal finances:

Tip One

Review your billing statement when you receive this information to ensure that the information contained within your statement is accurate and that there have been no changes made to the terms and conditions of your account.

Tip Two

Contact your creditor if you have any questions concerning your account. Stay in touch with your creditor if your financial situation has changed. Remember communication is key in solving problems before they occur. Be proactive about your credit account. Just remember no question is a dumb question! It's better to know then not to know information that you need instead of wondering what the answer is to the question you have not asked.

Tip Three

If you have a change in your income due to being laid off from your job, contact your creditors as soon as possible about the changes in your financial circumstances. By doing this you may be able to have your account payments reduced or deferred to assist you until you can get back on your feet. Don't keep your creditors in the dark about your situation. It's better to be proactive then reactive!

Tip Four

Make sure to check your credit line limits and interest rates on a monthly basis to see if there are any changes in these areas on your statements. You may be able to determine whether or not your credit limit has been reduced or if your interest rate has been increased.

Tip Five

Review all the mail you have received from your creditors! There may be important changes made to your account that may affect you. This may include notices concerning interest rate changes, credit limit reductions, credit lines being closed, terms and conditions of your accounts changing or any other information you may need to know.

Tip Six

Run your credit report or FICO score at least annually. You may even consider running your credit report and credit score twice a year. You are able to secure a credit report from the three credit reporting agencies annually for free at www.freeannualcreditreport.com.

So as you can see in order to attempt to maintain a balance with your creditors you will want to try to stay a few steps ahead of them if you can. By trying to be active when it comes to your credit you may be able to stay ahead of the continuous changes in the financial world that many of us face with our personal finances in today's economy. Just stay proactive when it comes to your personal finances so you have the ability to reduce or eliminate being reactive to changes that may occur to your credit.

Chapter 25
Conclusion

Hopefully you have been able to use the information provided to you in *Personal Finance Tips For You* as a tool to improve your personal finances. The chapters in this book have been created with you in mind.

As you strive to stay on track to improve your personal finances just keep in mind that you can do it if you just try. If you take the first initial step forward on working to improve your personal finances you will be in the position to achieve your present and future financial goals.

Once you get started in improving your own finances you should find out that this will make you feel much better and it will assist you in achieving perhaps other personal goals you have set for yourself and your family.

So, stay focused, persistent, determined and consistent and you should be on your way to staying in control of your personal finances.

REFERENCES

INTERNET WEBSITES

www.consumer.gov/idtheft
www.credit.com
www.equifax.com
www.experian.com
www.freeannualcreditreport.com
www.google.com
www.msn.com
www.pbgc.gov
www.prbc.com
www.rentbureau.com
www.transunion.com
www.yahoo.com

REFERENCES
TELEPHONE
NUMBERS

Certegy Inc. 800-437-5120
Equifax 800-685-1111
Equifax 800-525-6285, Fraud Unit
Experian 888-397-3742
Experian 888-397-3742, Fraud Unit
Hope Now Hotline at 888-995-HOPE or 888-995-4673
Scan 800-262-7771
TeleCheck 800-366-2425
TransUnion 800-916-8800
TransUnion 800-680-7289, Fraud Unit

About The Author

Nocita Carter has been part of the business and financial industry for over eighteen years and holds Masters' Degrees in Business Administration and Organizational Management from the University of Phoenix.

As an author I believe that I have been blessed with the gift of writing and it is my commitment and duty to share this talent by striving to provide useful tips and information on various topics that may help others in their current and future goals.

It is my sincere pleasure to share my knowledge with others that may find the information in my book useful to them. I have been actively writing over the years and currently reside in Temecula, California.

Index

D

E

payment methods, 36
Payment Reporting Builds Credit, 36
pension, 31–32
personal finance homework, 19, 22
personal finances, 1–1, 5, 9, 19, 23–24, 50, 54, 64, 72,
88–92

personal loans, 27
piggy bank, 54, 80
pre-employment process, 46
prime loans, 27
product choice, 83–84

R

rainy day, 60–64
rate, 3, 28, 36–38
rent, 36, 72, 91
report, 20, 42–46
retirement, 31–32, 67–68
retirement fund, 31, 68
retirement plan, 67
retirement planning, 67–68

S

savings, 6, 19–20, 24, 50–54, 63–64, 68, 79–80, 84
secured credit cards, 35–36
spare change, 79
spending, 5, 16, 20, 49–50, 63–64, 68
student loans, 71

7507022R0

Made in the USA
Charleston, SC
12 March 2011

TIPS AND TRICKS
FOR SERVING DIPS

Dips have progressed far beyond the standard on-
ion-sour cream dip. Now they can vary from very
simple to most elegant. Dips provide an ideal way to serve a large
number of guests for as little money as you choose to spend. They
are generally easy to prepare and easy to transport. Also, many
recipes can be made in advance. So take time to plan well, use
your imagination and present these dips with a flare!

NATURAL CONTAINERS FOR DIPS

Hollow out some of these items to make containers to hold
your dip for a unique presentation.

- honeydew melon
- melon
- bread loaf
- cantaloupe

- eggplant
- grapefruit
- cabbage
- lemon

- orange
- bell pepper
- zucchini
- pineapple

- pumpkin
- winter squash
- watermelon
- potato

IDEAS FOR DIPPERS FOR SAVORY DIPS

In addition to the usual chips and crackers, here is a list of ideas for dippers.

- crisp pita triangles
- bread sticks
- baguette bread rounds
- toast triangles
- pretzels
- small cooked new potatoes
- zucchini rounds
- Belgian endive

- yellow crookneck squash strips
- bell pepper strips
- carrot slices
- cabbage wedges
- cooked artichokes
- cauliflower florets
- jicama slices
- radishes

- cucumber slices
- celery
- cherry tomatoes with stems

- strips of beef, chicken or pork
- cooked prawns

IDEAS FOR DIPPERS FOR SWEET DIPS

- bite-sized chunks of fruit
- strawberries with stems
- pound cake chunks

- lady fingers
- other firm cookies
- dried fruits

WAYS TO REDUCE FAT IN DIP RECIPES

- Use low fat or nonfat cream cheese in place of whole cream cheese.
- Use nonfat sour cream or drained yogurt ("yogurt cheese") as a replacement for sour cream.
- Use low fat cottage cheese.
- Use low fat or nonfat cheeses.

- When frying in butter, use ½ butter and ½ unsaturated vegetable oil. This will not reduce fat, but will reduce cholesterol.
- When the recipe calls for frying in oil, substitute chicken stock or water.
- Substitute ground turkey in recipes calling for hamburger.

GARNISHES FOR DIPS

- strawberries
- beets (carved)
- berries
- onion flowers
- gherkins
- lettuce
- green onions
- lemon, lime or grapefruit slices, or baskets
- kale
- tomatoes
- mushrooms (fluted)
- grapes (fresh or frosted)
- pineapple wedges
- cilantro
- watercress
- parsley

HELPFUL HINTS

- When planning your menu, try to achieve a balance between taste, color, texture and temperature.

- Make some vegetarian and low fat dishes for health-conscious guests.

- If you have a guest with allergies you are aware of, avoid those ingredients if possible, or make a card listing the ingredients and place it by the food.

- There should be a minimum of 4 different types of appetizers available for a party of 20 guests. Allow at least 10 "bites" per person for a 2- to 3-hour party.

- Make sure the garnish is appropriate for the dish.

- Take a little extra time to prepare those finishing touches — presentation really makes a difference.

- Vary the dippers.

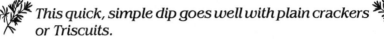

CRAB DIP

This quick, simple dip goes well with plain crackers or Triscuits.

2 cups fresh crabmeat
1/2 cup mayonnaise
1 can (8 oz.) water chestnuts, drained and
finely chopped
1-2 tbs. soy sauce
2 green onions, finely chopped
2 tbs. chopped fresh parsley
lemon juice to taste

Save a few pieces of crabmeat for garnish. Gently mix all ingredients together, taste and adjust quantity of lemon juice and soy sauce to taste.

Makes 3 cups

SAVORY COLD DIPS

HUMMUS DIP

This is a version of a garbanzo bean dip that originated in the Middle East. It's quick to put together and is ideally served with fresh or toasted pita bread. If you use canned garbanzos, rinse them with cold water and drain them well. Tahini is sesame seed paste, which greatly enhances the flavor but adds fat to the recipe.

1 tbs. olive oil
1 small onion, chopped
2-3 cloves garlic, minced
2 cups cooked chick peas
  (garbanzo beans)

½ tsp. turmeric
2 tbs. chopped fresh parsley
1-2 tbs. lemon juice, to taste
2-3 tbs. tahini, optional

Heat olive oil in a skillet and sauté onion and garlic until soft and transparent. Place all ingredients in a blender or food processor and puree until the consistency resembles that of mayonnaise.

Makes 3 cups

MANGO CHUTNEY DIP

This can be used as a dip or a spread. If you want a spread, do not add chutney to the recipe. Oil and fill a 3-cup mold, chill the mixture for several hours, unmold and drizzle chutney over the top.

12 oz. cream cheese,
  softened
3 tbs. mayonnaise
3 tbs. chopped peanuts
3-4 tbs. raisins
1 tbs. chopped green onions

3-4 slices bacon, fried crisp
  and crumbled
2 tsp. curry powder
1/2 cup shredded coconut
1 cup chopped mango chutney

In a food processor or blender, combine cream cheese and mayonnaise until smooth. Add remaining ingredients, adjusting the quantity of curry powder to your personal taste. If desired, reserve coconut to garnish top of dip.

Makes 10-12 servings

GUACAMOLE

Save the avocado pit and imbed it in the center of the mixture until ready to serve — this will help to keep the dip from becoming dark. Serve with tortilla chips, corn chips or plain tortillas.

4 large ripe avocados, peeled
  and pitted
juice of 2 limes
½ cup shredded cheddar
  cheese
½ cup chopped tomatoes
½ cup chopped Bermuda
  onion

dash salt
1 jalapeño pepper, chopped,
  optional
1 tbs. chopped cilantro,
  optional
chopped tomatoes or chopped
  cilantro for garnish

In a food processor or blender, blend avocados until smooth. Add remaining ingredients, taste and adjust seasonings to personal taste.

Makes 3 cups

SAVORY COLD DIPS

SALMON DIP

This deliciously simple recipe will create rave reviews. Serve with crackers, bread rounds or fresh vegetables for dipping.

8 oz. cream cheese, softened
1 can (1 lb.) salmon
2 tsp. minced onion
1 tbs. lemon juice
1 tbs. horseradish
1/4 tsp. salt

1/4 tsp. Liquid Smoke
1 tbs. chopped fresh parsley
milk to thin mixture, optional
chopped toasted pecans for
  garnish

With a mixer, beat cream cheese until smooth. Add salmon, onion, lemon juice, horseradish, salt, Liquid Smoke and parsley. If mixture appears too thick, add enough milk to thin mixture for easy dipping. Sprinkle top with toasted pecans.

Makes 2 1/2 cups

DILL DIP

This delicious dip goes well with a vegetable tray or potato chips. Beau monde seasoning is a blend of salt, sugar, onion and celery seed, and is available wherever spices and herbs are sold.

1 cup sour cream (can use nonfat)
1/3 cup mayonnaise
1 tbs. chopped green onion
1 tbs. chopped fresh parsley
1 tsp. dill
1 tsp. beau monde seasoning

Mix all ingredients together in a bowl and refrigerate for 2 to 3 hours before serving.

Makes 1 1/2 cups

THREE CHEESE DIP

For cheese lovers, this is a must. Serve with bread sticks or small rounds of rye bread.

½ cup butter, softened
¼ lb. Edam cheese
¼ lb. Parmesan cheese
¼ lb. Danish blue cheese, finely crumbled
1½ tsp. paprika
½ tsp. salt
⅓ cup sour cream (can use nonfat)

With a mixer, beat butter until smooth. Finely grate Edam cheese and add to butter with Parmesan, blue cheese, paprika and salt, mixing well. Gently stir in sour cream and serve.

Makes 2 cups

AVOCADO DIP

This is another simple dip that goes well with all types of chips. You can also use this as a spread for sandwiches. If you plan to store this dip, save the avocado pit and mix it in with the dip until ready to serve. This will help to keep the mixture from turning dark.

2 large ripe avocados, peeled and pitted
4 tsp. lemon juice
2 tsp. grated onion
1/2 cup sour cream, or mayonnaise
dash Tabasco Sauce
salt and pepper

Place all ingredients in a food processor or blender and beat until smooth. Taste and adjust seasonings.

Makes 1 1/2 cups

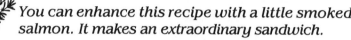

PIMIENTO CREAM CHEESE DIP

You can enhance this recipe with a little smoked salmon. It makes an extraordinary sandwich.

16 oz. cream cheese, softened
1/4 cup minced onion
4 tsp. lemon juice
4 chicken bouillon cubes
2/3 cup hot water
2 tbs. chopped pimiento
1/8 tsp. dill seed, optional

With a mixer, beat cream cheese until smooth. Beat in onion and lemon juice. Dissolve chicken bouillon cubes in hot water and beat into cream cheese mixture. Gently beat in pimiento and dill (if desired). Do not overmix.

Makes 2 2/3 cups

OLIVE APPETIZER DIP

This quick dip goes well with French bread, bread sticks or vegetable trays. Or spread it on rounds of French bread, sprinkle them with grated Swiss cheese and broil until bubbly.

1 avocado, peeled and pitted
1 tsp. lemon juice
1 cup finely chopped black
  olives
1/4 cup finely chopped red
  or green bell peppers

1/4 cup finely chopped tomatoes
1 tbs. finely chopped fresh
  parsley
8 oz. cream cheese, softened
1/4 cup finely chopped celery
  (for "crunch"), optional

Mash avocado with lemon juice. Using a mixer or stirring by hand, blend in remaining ingredients, making sure not to overmix so that vegetables remain somewhat intact. Chill until ready to serve.

Makes 3-3½ cups

VEGGIE DIP

This vegetable dip is similar to a very creamy vinaigrette.

1 tbs. Dijon mustard
1½ tbs. vinegar (prefer balsamic)
1½ tbs. lemon juice
1 tsp. salt
pepper
pinch sugar

½ cup olive oil
1 large ripe avocado, peeled and pitted
8 oz. cream cheese
1-2 cloves garlic, minced
2-3 tbs. minced green onion
2 tbs. minced fresh parsley

Place Dijon mustard, vinegar, lemon juice, salt, pepper and sugar in a blender or food processor and process until well mixed. Slowly pour olive oil in a fine stream into mustard mixture, allowing it to emulsify. Add remaining ingredients, taste and adjust seasonings.

Makes 2½ cups

PECAN CHEESE DIP

This somewhat strange combination is especially a favorite of men. Great with crackers, bread or even as a dip for meats.

8 oz. cream cheese
1 cup chopped toasted pecans
2 tbs. steak sauce
1 clove garlic, minced
few drops Tabasco Sauce
enough milk to thin mixture

Place all ingredients except milk in a food processor or blender and process until just mixed. Add milk a few tablespoons at a time to thin to the consistency you desire.

Makes 2 cups

CURRY VEGGIE DIP

This dip can be used with vegetable trays and also for dipping cooked meats like chicken and beef strips. Serve it in a hollowed-out green vegetable, such as a large zucchini, for a beautiful contrast.

3 cups mayonnaise
2 tbs. finely chopped onion
2 tsp. curry powder, or to taste
1 tsp. dry mustard
few drops Tabasco Sauce
1 tsp. salt
pepper

Place all ingredients in a food processor or blender and process until smooth. Taste and adjust seasonings. Refrigerate until ready to use.

Makes 3 cups

COTTAGE CLAM DIP

This is a relatively low fat dip that goes well with hearty crackers or chips.

1 cup creamed cottage cheese (low fat can be used)
6 drops Tabasco Sauce, or to taste
$\frac{1}{2}$ tsp. Worcestershire sauce
$\frac{1}{2}$ tsp. onion salt
$\frac{1}{4}$ tsp. salt
1 tbs. clam juice
1 can (6 oz.) minced clams, drained, liquid reserved

Place cottage cheese, Tabasco, Worcestershire, onion salt, salt and reserved clam juice in a food processor or blender and process until smooth. (Add more clam juice if you prefer a thinner consistency.) Stir in clams and refrigerate until ready to serve.

Makes 1$\frac{1}{2}$ cups

DEVILED HAM DIP

This dip has a little change from the ordinary with the addition of apple. Serve with toasted bread rounds.

1 cup cooked ham
1 green bell pepper, minced
1 large tart apple, chopped
¼ cup diced sweet pickle
½ cup mayonnaise

½ tsp. dry mustard
¼ tsp. salt
dash Tabasco Sauce, or
  cayenne pepper

Place ham, green pepper, apple and pickle in a food processor or blender and process until finely minced. Add remaining ingredients and process until just mixed. Add more mayonnaise if you desire a thinner consistency. Taste and adjust seasonings. Refrigerate until ready to use.

Makes 2¾ cups

AVOCADO CRAB DIP

This creamy, delicate dip is ideally served with plain crackers or melba toast.

2 ripe avocados, peeled and pitted
1/4 cup lemon juice
8 oz. cream cheese, softened
2 tsp. minced onion
salt and pepper
milk to thin mixture
2 cans (6 oz. each) crabmeat

Place avocados and lemon juice in a food processor or blender and process until avocados are pureed. Add cream cheese, onion, salt and pepper to avocado mixture and blend until smooth. Add milk a few tablespoons at a time until you reach the desired consistency. Gently stir in crabmeat. Taste and adjust seasonings. Refrigerate until ready to use.

Makes 2 1/2-3 cups

CHUTNEY AND SHRIMP DIP

This dip is best with crackers, but also good with crunchy fresh vegetable dippers. Garnish the top with a sprinkling of chopped fresh parsley.

8 oz. cream cheese, softened
2 tsp. curry powder
1/2 tsp. crushed garlic
1/4 cup mango chutney
1/3 tsp. salt
1 cup chopped cooked shrimp
1/2 cup sour cream
chopped fresh parsley for garnish

Beat cream cheese, curry powder, garlic, chutney and salt together until well mixed. Fold in shrimp and sour cream. Garnish with parsley. Refrigerate until ready to serve.

Makes 3 cups

GINGER SESAME DIP

Try this great dip with skewered meat, especially chicken.

2 cups sour cream
2½ tbs. soy sauce
4 tsp. Worcestershire sauce
1 tsp. ground ginger
2 tbs. toasted sesame seeds

Stir all ingredients together. Taste and adjust seasonings. Refrigerate for several hours before serving.

Makes 2½ cups

Just O.K.

SUN-DRIED TOMATO AND BEAN DIP

This easy no-bake bean dip with an Italian flare is best served with bread sticks. If your sun-dried tomatoes are dry-packed, rather than packed in a jar in oil, reconstitute them in water before draining and chopping.

2 cans (15 oz. each) white beans
1/3 cup drained chopped sun-dried tomatoes
2 tbs. chopped fresh basil
2 tbs. olive oil
2 tsp. minced garlic
1/4 tsp. salt, or more to taste
1/8 tsp. pepper

Drain beans and rinse. Place all ingredients in a food processor or blender and process until well mixed but not completely mashed. Taste and adjust seasonings. Cover and refrigerate until ready to use.

Makes 2 cups

ROASTED RED PEPPER DIP

Here is another excellent dip to serve with fresh vegetables. Cut the top off a red bell pepper, remove the seeds and fill it with this mixture to serve.

1 jar (15 oz.) roasted red bell peppers, drained
2 green onions, cut into fine pieces
1-2 tbs. lemon juice
1 cup whipped cream cheese

Place all ingredients in a food processor or blender and process into a coarse puree. Chill before serving.

Makes 2½ cups

SWEET POTATO AND CARROT DIP

Dip into this piquant yet sweet vegetable dip with vegetables or pita bread. For a healthy alternative, rather than boiling the vegetables, steam them until tender and add a sprinkling of salt for flavor.

1 lb. sweet potatoes or yams
1 lb. carrots
water to cover
1 tsp. salt
3 cloves garlic
1 tsp. ground cumin
1 tsp. cinnamon
3-4 tbs. olive oil
3 tbs. vinegar (prefer balsamic)
pinch cayenne pepper, or more to taste

Peel sweet potatoes (or yams) and carrots and cut into pieces. Place in a saucepan, cover with water, add salt and boil until vegetables are soft. Drain. Puree cooked vegetables in a food processor or blender until smooth. Add remaining ingredients and puree until blended. Taste and adjust seasonings to your personal preference.

Makes 4 cups

EGGPLANT CAVIAR

This great, all-vegetable dip is even better served in a hollowed-out eggplant.

2 eggplants
1 tbs. olive oil
2 cloves garlic
1 small onion
1 red bell pepper, seeded
1 green bell pepper, seeded
1 tomato, peeled and seeded
2 tsp. capers
1 tbs. fresh lemon juice

1/8 tsp. Tabasco Sauce
1 tsp. salt
1/4 tsp. pepper
3 tbs. vinegar (prefer balsamic)
1 tsp. basil
1/4 cup olive oil
1/2 cup chopped black olives
1/2 cup chopped green olives

Brush eggplants with olive oil and bake in a 350° oven for 30 minutes (or until they begin to soften). Remove from oven, cut in half and scoop out flesh. Save the eggplant shell if you wish to serve the dip in it. In a food processor or blender, chop garlic. Add onion and bell peppers. Pulse on and off to coarsely chop vegetables. Remove chopped vegetables and set aside. Add tomato, eggplant pulp, capers, lemon juice, Tabasco, salt, pepper, vinegar, basil and oil to processor or blender and process until well mixed. Add coarsely chopped vegetables and process just until mixed. Transfer vegetables to a heavy saucepan and cook over medium heat for 20 minutes. Add chopped olives, taste and adjust seasonings, and chill. Serve in a hollowed-out eggplant shell or colorful dish.

Makes 1 quart

TAPENADE (OLIVE DIP)

This is a perfect dip to take to a party. Cut little baguettes into small rounds for dipping, or use bread sticks.

2 cans (6 oz. each) pitted black olives
3 tbs. capers
1/2 cup minced onion
1 tsp. minced garlic
2 tbs. chopped fresh parsley
1/4 cup grated Parmesan cheese
2 tbs. olive oil
2 tbs. vinegar (prefer balsamic)
1/2 tsp. salt
1/2 tsp. pepper
4 tbs. chopped red bell pepper

With a food processor or blender, just barely chop olives; remove and set aside. Put remaining ingredients into processor except 2 tbs. red bell pepper. Chop into a fine blend and stir this mixture into olives. Taste and adjust seasonings. Sprinkle remaining chopped red pepper on top for garnish.

Makes 3 cups

SPINACH DIP

This is an old favorite. If you use nonfat sour cream and mayonnaise, it's perfect for serving to health-conscious guests who also like delicious food. This recipe will keep for about 2 days.

1 pint sour cream (can use nonfat)
1 cup mayonnaise (can use low fat or nonfat)
¾ pkg. (1.8 oz.) dried leek soup mix
1 pkg. (10 oz.) frozen spinach
½ cup chopped fresh parsley
½ cup chopped green onion
1 tsp. dill
1 tsp. dry Italian salad seasoning mix

In a bowl, stir sour cream, mayonnaise and leek soup mix together. Defrost spinach and squeeze out all excess liquid. Add spinach to sour cream mixture and stir well. Add remaining ingredients and stir. Refrigerate for several hours to allow flavors to mellow.

Makes 5 cups

SALSA

It's a must to serve salsa with tortilla chips (freshly made if you've got the time). It's also good with bean dishes, vegetable salads and chicken.

1 medium sweet onion
3 cloves garlic, crushed
½ green bell pepper, chopped
½ red bell pepper, chopped
½ cup chopped cilantro
2 tbs. lemon juice
2 tsp. sugar
1 can (15 oz.) Mexican-style stewed tomatoes
salt and pepper
chopped fresh jalapeño chiles, optional

Place all ingredients in a food processor or blender. Process with pulsing action until blended. Taste and adjust seasoning .

Makes 2½ cups

ASPARAGUS MAYO DIP

This recipe makes a good alternative dip for vegetable trays or as a dipping sauce for artichokes. Use it as a dressing for vegetable pasta salad that has chopped asparagus as one of the ingredients.

1 cup finely chopped asparagus	salt and pepper
4 egg yolks	1 tbs. vinegar
1 tbs. dry mustard	1½ cups vegetable oil

Steam asparagus until tender and process in a blender or food processor to a smooth puree. You should have about ½ cup puree. Allow puree to cool. In a food processor or blender, place egg yolks, mustard, salt, pepper and vinegar and mix thoroughly. Add oil in a thin stream while food processor or blender is running, until it has all been added and mixture is smooth and thick. Add asparagus puree to mixture and blend until well mixed. Refrigerate until ready to use.

Makes 2½ cups

MIXED CHEESE DIP

Quick, simple and delicious!

8 oz. cream cheese, softened
½ lb. butter, softened
2 jars (5 oz. each) pimiento cheese spread
1 jar (5 oz.) Roquefort cheese spread
1 jar (5 oz.) Old English cheese spread
1 cup grated cheddar cheese
dash salt
dash Worcestershire sauce
few drops Tabasco Sauce
⅓-½ cup cream or milk

Place all ingredients in a food processor or blender and process until smooth. Add enough cream or milk to make a good dipping consistency. Taste and adjust seasonings to your personal preference.

Makes 5 cups

APRICOT CHUTNEY DIP

Put this dip on your buffet table surrounded by bite-sized chunks of fresh fruit on picks. This somewhat sweet dip can also be served with crackers. It is delicious as a sauce over chopped fruit.

8 oz. cream cheese
4-5 tbs. apricot chutney
¾ tsp. curry powder
½ cup toasted coconut
milk to thin mixture

Place cream cheese, chutney, curry powder and coconut in a food processor or blender and mix until blended. Add milk a few tablespoons at a time until you reach a dipping consistency.

Makes 1½ cups

CREAMY PECAN DIP

This is an incredible dip that uses a unique combination of creamy ingredients finished off with toasted pecans. It is appreciated by adults and children both. Serve it with a fruit tray. It also makes a really wonderful dressing for fruit salads.

8 oz. cream cheese, softened
1 jar (7 oz.) marshmallow creme
1 container (8 oz.) Cool Whip
2 cups vanilla yogurt
1 cup chopped toasted pecans

With a mixer, whip cream cheese until soft. Add marshmallow creme and blend until smooth. Gently fold in Cool Whip and vanilla yogurt until mixed. Chill until ready to use. Just before serving, stir in toasted pecans.

Makes 7-8 cups

FRUIT CUSTARD DIP

This is another favorite dip for fruits or to use as a dressing on fruit salads. This can be stored for days.

1 cup orange juice
2 cups pineapple juice
1 cup sugar
1/3 cup cornstarch
enough cold water to make a paste
2 tbs. butter

Place orange juice, pineapple juice and sugar in a saucepan and bring to a boil. Mix cornstarch with enough water to make a paste and stir this into hot juice mixture. Continue to stir until mixture thickens. Watch carefully that you do not scorch. Remove from heat, add butter and stir until butter melts. Cool completely before using.

Makes 4 cups

PINEAPPLE-ORANGE YOGURT DIP

You can't go wrong with the combination of pine-apple and orange. It makes a great dip for fruit, fruit salad dressing and even spooned on top of granola. If you aren't crazy about coconut, use chopped toasted almonds.

1 can (8¼ oz.) crushed pineapple, drained
8 oz. orange yogurt
4 oz. whipped cream cheese
¼ cup toasted coconut
2 tbs. brown sugar, or to taste
milk to thin mixture, optional

Mix all ingredients together with a mixer. If desired, add a little milk to thin mixture. Chill for several hours before serving.

Makes 3 cups

CREAMY BERRY DIP

This is a great dessert dip that utilizes frozen berries, so it can be made any time of year. It goes particularly well with cake cubes. This is especially good if you use the liqueur to match the type of berries you use — such as framboise with frozen raspberries.

1 lb. cream cheese, softened
4 tbs. berry liqueur or brandy
2 pkg. (10 oz. each) frozen berries, thawed
sugar, optional

In a heavy saucepan, mix cream cheese and liqueur together and melt over low heat. Add berries to saucepan, stirring until berries are heated through. Taste and determine whether or not you wish to add sugar. Stir gently until sugar is dissolved. Refrigerate until ready to serve.

Makes 4 cups

STRAWBERRY GINGER
DIPPING SAUCE

This creamy fruit sauce goes well with fruit such as bananas, strawberries and grapes. It is best to chill overnight so the flavor can develop. Pour this sauce over chopped fruit and serve as a breakfast fruit or a fruit dessert.

2 tbs. chopped crystallized ginger
1 cup sour cream
½ cup strawberries
1 medium banana
1 tbs. light brown sugar
1 tbs. rum

In a food processor or blender, process crystallized ginger until finely chopped. Add remaining ingredients and blend until smooth. Chill for at least 3 hours before serving.

Makes 2 cups

HOT NACHOS DIP

This delicious Mexican-type dish is perfect to take to parties. It is easy to prepare and there is never any left. Serve it with tortilla chips.

½ lb. lean ground beef
½ lb. sausage (chorizo or hot Italian variety)
1 large onion, chopped
salt
1 can (1 lb.) refried beans
1 can (4 oz.) chopped green chiles (mild or hot)
2-3 cups shredded cheddar cheese
¾ cup taco sauce (mild or hot)
1 cup sour cream
1 can (6 oz.) frozen avocado dip, thawed
1 cup chopped black olives
¼ cup chopped green onions

In a skillet, crumble ground beef and sausage and cook until just brown. Drain off fat. Add onion and cook until wilted. Add salt to taste. Spread refried beans in a large, low-sided baking dish and cover with cooked meat mixture. Sprinkle with chopped green chiles, top with shredded cheese and drizzle with taco sauce. Bake uncovered in a 400° oven for 20 to 25 minutes. Remove from oven and spread with sour cream. Mound avocado dip in the center (or gently spread over sour cream). Sprinkle with olives and green onions. Serve hot.

Makes 8 servings

HOT CLAM DIP

Instead of the common onion dip, consider using clam dip with a little tang of hot pepper sauce. Serve with crackers or French bread rounds.

8 oz. cream cheese, softened
1 cup grated mild cheddar cheese
1 tbs. lemon juice, or more to taste
1 tsp. Worcestershire sauce
2 cloves garlic, minced
½ tsp. hot pepper sauce
½ tsp. salt
½ cup minced onion
3 tbs. minced parsley
2 cans (7 oz. each) minced clams, drained, juice reserved
3 tbs. clam juice, or more if necessary
grated cheddar cheese for garnish
chopped parsley for garnish

Combine cream cheese, cheddar cheese, lemon juice, Worcestershire, garlic, hot pepper sauce and salt. Stir minced onion and parsley into cream cheese mixture. Add clams and 3 tbs. clam juice and stir. Add more clam juice if a thinner consistency is desired. Just barely heat in a casserole dish or chafing dish and serve. Garnish with a little grated cheddar cheese and sprinkle with chopped parsley.

Makes 3 cups

HOT CRAB DIP

An expensive dip, this can be reserved for special occasions. Although you may use canned crab, fresh is better. Stand 3 leg pieces in a cluster of parsley for a beautiful garnish. Serve with Triscuits, other crackers or vegetables for dipping.

16 oz. cream cheese
1/4 cup finely chopped onions
2-3 tbs. milk
1 tsp. horseradish
1/2 tsp. salt
dash white pepper
1 lb. fresh or canned crabmeat
crab legs (if available) for garnish
fresh parsley or toasted
slivered almonds for garnish

Mix all ingredients together except crabmeat and garnishes. Mixture should be smooth. Heat mixture gently in a chafing dish or fondue pot. Just before serving, gently stir in crabmeat, trying not to break up crabmeat too much. Garnish with crab legs if possible, and parsley or a sprinkling of toasted almonds.

Makes 4 cups

SOUTH-OF-THE-BORDER DIP

*You can make this dip a vegetarian one by elimi-
nating the ground beef and using vegetarian refried
beans. Serve with tortillas or corn chips. Or consider making your own chips by cutting corn tortillas into
wedges, deep fat frying until crisp and draining on paper towels.*

1 lb. lean ground beef
2 cans (16 oz. each) refried beans
1 pkg. (2.25 oz.) taco seasoning mix
2 cups shredded cheddar or Jack cheese
1/2 cup finely chopped onions
4-6 drops Tabasco Sauce
enough milk or water to thin mixture, optional
chopped green onions for garnish

In a large skillet, cook meat until brown and drain off any excess fat. Add remaining ingredients and stir until well mixed. If mixture appears too thick, add a little milk or water to thin. Serve in a chafing dish, fondue pot or slow cooking pot to keep warm and sprinkle top with a small amount of chopped green onions.

Makes 6 cups

HOT ARTICHOKE DIP

This incredibly rich hot dip is best served with thin crackers or French bread rounds.

2 cans (8½ oz. each) artichoke hearts
1 cup mayonnaise
1 cup sour cream
2 cups grated Parmesan cheese
1 cup chopped water chestnuts
1-2 green onions, finely chopped

Cut artichoke hearts into small pieces. Combine with remaining ingredients, mix well and place in a baking dish. Bake at 350° for 35 minutes. Keep warm while serving.

Makes 7-8 cups

CREAMY HOT CRAB DIP

Here is another version of a crab dip, creamy, old-fashioned and wonderful. The paprika adds color. Serve with French bread or plain crackers.

2 tbs. butter
2 oz. mushrooms, sliced
½ tsp. lemon juice
3 egg yolks
1 cup cream

4 tbs. sweet sherry
salt and pepper
dash cayenne pepper
paprika
1 lb. fresh crabmeat

In a saucepan, melt butter and sauté mushrooms until tender, adding lemon juice to help prevent mushrooms from darkening. Beat egg yolks together, add cream and stir. Add sherry, salt, pepper, cayenne and paprika; stir until smooth. Add crabmeat just before serving. Serve warm.

Makes 3 cups

SWEET AND SOUR DIPPING SAUCE

This sauce can be used with all kinds of meat for dipping, such as cooked chicken, rumaki, barbecued pork, fried prawns and even cooked pork.

1½ tbs. cornstarch
¾ cup pineapple juice
½ cup brown sugar
1 tsp. salt
½ cup cider vinegar
4 tsp. ketchup
1 cup drained crushed pineapple
2 drops red food coloring, optional

Mix cornstarch with pineapple juice and bring to a boil. Add brown sugar, salt, vinegar, ketchup, crushed pineapple and red food coloring (if desired). Stir until thickened. Serve warm.

Makes 2 cups

SEAFOOD CHEDDAR DIP

Like many dips, this one is extremely simple and quick to prepare. Serve with mild crackers or thinly sliced French bread.

12 oz. cream cheese, softened
8 oz. sour cream
onion or garlic salt
white pepper
1 cup shrimp or crabmeat
1 cup shredded cheddar cheese

In a bowl, mix together cream cheese, sour cream, onion or garlic salt and pepper until mixture is smooth. Gently fold in shrimp or crabmeat. Place mixture in a small, shallow baking dish. Sprinkle with cheddar cheese. Bake in a 350° oven for 20 minutes.

Makes 4 cups

CREAMY HAMBURGER DIP

Here's a dip for those times when you need a protein-rich appetizer and want an alternative to chicken wings. Serve with hearty crackers, chips, toasted bread fingers or cooked new potatoes. Sugar is added to remove the slight bitterness that garlic and tomatoes may impart.

1 lb. extra lean ground beef, or ground turkey
½ cup chopped onions
garlic salt
¼ cup ketchup
1 can (8 oz.) tomato sauce
8 oz. cream cheese
⅓-¼ cup grated Parmesan cheese
¾ tsp. oregano
1 tsp. sugar

Cook hamburger, onions and garlic salt in a skillet until onions are wilted. Add remaining ingredients and cook on low for ½ hour. Serve hot in a chafing dish.

Makes 4-5 cups

JALAPEÑO BEAN DIP

The quantity of jalapeños will totally determine the heat, so be careful or go wild! Serve with chips or toast triangles.

2½ cups cooked pinto beans, or canned,
rinsed and drained
1-6 jalapeño chiles
1 tbs. olive oil
½ tsp. salt, or to taste
½ tsp. oregano
¼ tsp. garlic powder

Mash pinto beans well and place in a saucepan. Cut tops off jalapeños, leaving them whole with seeds inside. Add remaining ingredients and simmer over low heat for 15 minutes. If mixture appears too thick, add water until the proper consistency is reached. Remove jalapeños and cool before serving.

Makes 2¾ cups

CHILI CON QUESO

This creamy, piquant dip deserves the extra effort of making homemade tortilla chips. Also good as a sauce for chicken, eggs, fish or pasta.

1 small onion, minced
2 tbs. butter
1 cup drained canned tomatoes
1 can (4 oz.) chopped mild
  green chiles
4 oz. cheddar cheese, grated

4 oz. Monterey Jack cheese,
  grated
1 cup cream
salt and pepper

In a saucepan, sauté onion in butter until soft. Chop tomatoes and add to saucepan with chiles. Simmer for 15 minutes. Add grated cheeses and stir until cheese melts. Gradually stir in cream until mixture is smooth. Season to taste. Serve hot in a chafing dish.

Makes 3 cups

PORK AND BEAN DIP

A slightly different version of a bean dip, this one hints of barbecued beans. Good with crisp pita triangles, chips or bread sticks.

1 can (16 oz.) pork and beans
1 can (8 oz.) tomato sauce
1/2 cup grated sharp cheddar cheese
1 tsp. garlic salt
1/2 tsp. salt
1 tsp. chili powder
2 tsp. vinegar
2 tsp. Worcestershire sauce
1/4-1/2 tsp. Liquid Smoke
dash Tabasco Sauce, or cayenne pepper
1/2 cup crumbled fried bacon for garnish

Place all ingredients in a heavy saucepan and warm until cheese is melted. Leave texture as is, or place all ingredients, except bacon, in a food processor or blender and process until smooth. Sprinkle bacon pieces on top for garnish.

Makes 3½ cups

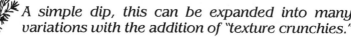

HOT PIMIENTO CHEESE DIP

A simple dip, this can be expanded into many variations with the addition of "texture crunchies."

1 lb. cheddar cheese, grated
1 can (12 oz.) evaporated milk
1 jar (4 oz.) chopped pimientos, drained
½ cup finely chopped raw vegetables
or
½ cup chopped black or green olives
or
½ cup crispy bacon bits
or
¼ cup chopped green onions

In a heavy saucepan or double boiler, melt cheese and evaporated milk together over low heat, stirring until smooth. Add pimiento and, if desired, any "crunchy" of choice. Serve in a chafing dish.

Makes 3 cups

CHEESY BEAN DIP

This dish is quick and always a hit because it is so flavorful. Serve with taco chips or bread rounds.

8 oz. cream cheese, softened
1 can (10 oz.) bean dip
1 cup sour cream
10-20 drops Tabasco Sauce
1/4 cup chopped green onions, or more to taste
1/2 pkg. (2.25 oz.) taco seasoning mix
4 oz. Jack cheese, shredded
4 oz. cheddar cheese, shredded

Mix all ingredients together except shredded cheeses. Place in a shallow casserole dish. Finish by covering with shredded cheeses. Bake in a 350° oven for 20 minutes. Serve hot.

Makes 6-8 servings

TEX-MEX DIP

No baking is required for this delicious dish. If you wish to make it totally vegetarian, make sure that the bean dip is made without animal fat. Serve with tortilla chips, or for a change try using blue corn tortilla chips.

3 ripe avocados, peeled and pitted
2 tbs. lemon juice
½ tsp. salt
2 cups sour cream
½ cup mayonnaise
1 pkg. (2.25 oz.) taco seasoning
2 cans (10 oz. each) bean dip
1 bunch green onions, chopped
1-2 tomatoes, diced
2 cans (6 oz.) olives, drained and chopped
8 oz. sharp cheddar cheese, shredded

With a food processor, blender or mixer, mix avocados with lemon juice and salt until smooth. Layer this on the bottom of a shallow serving dish. Stir sour cream, mayonnaise and taco seasoning mix together and gently spread sour cream mixture over avocado mixture. Mix bean dip, green onions, tomatoes and olives together and spread this over sour cream mixture. Sprinkle with cheddar cheese and serve.

Makes 8-10 servings

CHILI DIP

This quick, easy-to-fix dish goes best with chips, bread sticks or celery sticks.

8 oz. cream cheese, softened
1 can (8 oz.) no-bean canned chili
1 can (4 oz.) chopped green chiles
1 cup grated cheddar cheese

Spread cream cheese on the bottom of a pie plate. Cover with chili and sprinkle with green chiles. Cover with cheddar cheese and bake 325° for 15 to 20 minutes.

Makes 3 cups

HOT MANGO SAUCE

Mango has an exotic flavor that complements meat beautifully. Serve this with chunks of pork, beef, fish or chicken.

3 mangoes, peeled and seeded
1 tbs. Madeira wine
⅓ cup melted butter
2-3 green chile peppers, seeded, finely diced
salt and pepper
1 tsp. caraway seeds, optional
water to thin sauce, optional

Place mangoes in a food processor or blender and puree until smooth. Add Madeira and mix well. Place all ingredients except caraway in a saucepan and simmer for 10 minutes. Taste and add caraway seeds (if desired). If mixture appears too thick, thin with a little water.

Makes 2¼ cups

SAVORY CHERRY DIPPING SAUCE

Dip pork or more exotic meats, such as duck or barbecued pork, into this sauce.

1½ cups drained canned
  pitted cherries
¾ cup corn syrup
½ cup vinegar
¼ tsp. cinnamon

⅛ tsp. nutmeg
pinch ground cloves
salt
pepper

Place all ingredients in a saucepan and bring to a boil. Reduce heat and simmer for about 5 minutes. Depending on the texture that appeals to you, keep cherries whole, partially grind in a food processor to leave some chunks for texture, or thoroughly puree and sieve for a fine sauce. Taste and adjust seasonings.

Makes 2¾ cups

CREAMY TUNA DIP

Serve this dip warm from a chafing dish. If you use cayenne pepper for garnish, you will add a little heat to the dish; paprika only adds color. It's good with chips or bread rounds.

8 oz. cream cheese
2 tbs. bottled chili sauce
1 jar (5 oz.) sharp processed cheese spread
2-3 tbs. chopped green onions
1 can (6½ oz.) tuna, drained
milk to thin mixture
cayenne pepper or paprika for garnish

Place cream cheese, chili sauce and processed cheese in a saucepan over low heat and stir until melted and smooth. Add green onions, tuna and enough milk to thin. Stir until mixed. Garnish with cayenne pepper or paprika. Serve warm.

Makes 2¼ cups

HOT ANCHOVY DIP

This Italian favorite is commonly known as bagna caôda, and is served barely warm. Traditional dippers are raw vegetables and bread.

1½ cups olive oil
6 tbs. butter
1½ tbs. minced garlic
18 flat anchovy fillets, chopped
1 tsp. salt, or to taste
dash Tabasco Sauce

Heat olive oil and butter together in a saucepan until they just begin to foam. Immediately toss in minced garlic and sauté very briefly (don't let it brown). Reduce heat and add anchovies to "wilted" garlic, stirring until anchovies dissolve into a paste. Add salt and Tabasco, if desired, and transfer mixture to a warming dish.

Makes 2 cups

HEARTY ITALIAN DIPPING SAUCE

This is very fast and easy to make. You can always experiment with herbs like oregano and basil for subtle changes. Serve with bread sticks or bread cubes for dipping.

½ lb. lean ground beef
2 cups spaghetti sauce
1½ cups grated cheddar cheese
1½ cups shredded mozzarella cheese
½ cup dry red wine, or more to thin mixture

In a skillet, brown ground beef. Drain off excess fat. Stir in spaghetti sauce and cheeses until thoroughly melted. Add wine and transfer mixture to a chafing dish to serve.

Makes 5 cups

HOT FUDGE DIPPING SAUCE

This is a great sauce for dipping pieces of pound cake, angel food cake or fruits like bananas, pears and apples.

4 oz. unsweetened chocolate
4 tbs. butter
4 tbs. light corn syrup
2 cups cream
2 cups sugar
4 tsp. vanilla extract
¼ tsp. salt

Grate chocolate into a heavy saucepan and melt with butter and corn syrup, stirring constantly over low heat. When chocolate is melted, add cream and sugar and cook until sugar is dissolved. Bring to a boil over moderate heat and boil without stirring for 8 minutes. Remove pan from heat and stir in vanilla and salt.

Makes 3 cups

JELLY FRUIT DIP

This can be served warm like a fondue for dipping fruits such as bananas, pineapple, melons or dried fruits. It can also be chilled and used as a dip for a fruit tray, in which case you may want to thin with additional orange juice.

1/4 cup cornstarch
6 tbs. sugar
1 1/2 cups cold water
1 cup currant jelly

1/2 cup sweet sherry
1/2 cup orange juice
6-7 tbs. lemon juice, or to
   taste

Place cornstarch, sugar and water in a saucepan and bring to a boil. Cook until mixture is thickened and sugar is dissolved. Add remaining ingredients and stir until smooth.

Makes 4 cups

CARAMEL DIPPING SAUCE

This popular flavor makes a delicious sauce for dipping fruits or cake pieces. Keep warm in a chafing dish.

1 cup sugar
½ cup water
⅓ cup heavy cream
4 tbs. butter, optional

Combine sugar and water in a small saucepan. Wash down any crystals on the sides of the pan with a pastry brush dipped in water, and bring to a boil. Cook gently without stirring until liquid is a deep golden brown. Remove pan from heat and carefully whisk in cream, a little at a time. If you want an even richer sauce, add butter and whisk until butter melts and mixture is smooth.

Makes 2 cups

LEMON DESSERT DIPPING SAUCE

Here's a delicious sauce for dipping fruits, pound cake, angel food cake, sponge cake or even lemon tea bread.

6 tbs. butter
1 cup sugar
1 tbs. grated lemon zest (colored peel
without white membrane)
¼ cup lemon juice
1 egg, beaten

Melt butter in a saucepan and gradually stir in remaining ingredients. Cook over medium heat until just before it begins to boil. Immediately remove from heat. Serve warm.

Makes 1½ cups

ENGLISH DESSERT SAUCE

Serve this rich, thick vanilla dessert sauce with chunks of cake or fruit. Create other sauce flavors from this base recipe by substituting flavored liqueurs in the place of vanilla extract.

8 egg yolks
1 cup sugar
1½ cups cream

1 cup milk
1-2 tsp. vanilla extract, to taste

With a mixer, beat egg yolks and sugar together until mixture is thick and pale yellow. Add cream and milk; mix until smooth. Pour into a heavy-bottomed saucepan and cook over medium heat, stirring constantly, until mixture thickens and coats the back of a spoon. Remove from heat and stir in vanilla extract or liqueur of choice. (A whisk produces a smoother sauce.) If desired, strain through a sieve. Serve either warm or cooled.

Makes 4 cups

HOT RASPBERRY LIQUEUR CREAM

Serve this flavorful sauce with fresh berries, pound cake, chocolate cake or crisp cookies for dipping.

8 egg yolks
1¾ cups raspberry liqueur
¼ cup sugar, or more to taste

Beat all ingredients together and place in a heavy-bottomed saucepan or double boiler. Continually whisk over medium heat until mixture becomes very thick (about 20 minutes). Serve warm.

Makes 3 cups

INDEX